MW01257507

At David C Cook, we equip the local church around the corner and around the globe to make disciples. Come see how we are working together—go to **www.davidccook.org**. Thank you!

transforming lives together

A **THRIVE**MOMS BIBLE STUDY

Abundance

DISCOVERING A FULL LIFE IN CHRIST

Kara-Kae James
& Ali Pedersen

DAVID C COOK
transforming lives together

ABUNDANCE
Published by David C Cook
4050 Lee Vance Drive
Colorado Springs, CO 80918 U.S.A.

Integrity Music Limited, a Division of David C Cook
Brighton, East Sussex BN1 2RE, England

The graphic circle C logo is a registered trademark of David C Cook.

ISBN 978-0-8307-7309-1
eISBN 978-0-8307-7912-3

© 2019 Kara-Kae James
The Author is represented by Alive Literary Agency, 7680 Goddard Street, Suite 200, Colorado Springs, CO 80920, www.aliveliterary.com.

Cowritten by Ali Pedersen
The Team: Alice Crider, Laura Derico, Amy Konyndyk, Nick Lee, Jack Campbell, Susan Murdock
Cover Design: Jon Middel

Printed in the United States of America
First Edition 2019

1 2 3 4 5 6 7 8 9 10

061919

CONTENTS

HOW TO USE THIS STUDY

Before you dive in, think about this question: What do you hope to get out of this study? (Write your answer below.)

Welcome to this Thrive Moms Bible study! Thrive Moms (www.thrivemoms.com) is a ministry that exists to encourage and inspire moms everywhere to do more than just *survive* motherhood. We want you to thrive, and we believe thriving happens when you connect with God's Word and one another.

This Bible study can be done as an individual or with a group. But we know we are always better together! Even if you grab just one friend to walk through the study with you, you'll stay on track better and keep each other accountable.

There are six weeks of study, and each week has four days (to not overwhelm you). Do these day studies at the times that work best for you. Each study week includes these features:

- Go to the Word sections to offer specific Bible verses to focus on.
- Simple questions to help you process the Bible passages.

- Space provided for you to make your own connections.
- Prayer suggestions to lead into your personal time with God.

Each week wraps up with a group discussion option, designed to offer time to talk over what you've learned from God's Word through the week, to share your experiences, and to learn from and encourage one another.

Prepare yourself with time and accountability as you begin. We are cheering you on into abundance as you study!

GROUP DISCUSSION GROUND RULES

SAFE SPACE

You are entering a safe space here, and it will all be worth it. Allow yourself to break down some walls and trust the women God has placed around you. Be honest and trustworthy with others. A key part of your personal growth is found in community with others. Be intentional in your conversation and the way you process Scripture.

COMMITMENT

Commit to do the work! We have made the study sessions intentionally short so that they are not overly time consuming. (They were written for busy moms!) Whether you are doing the study on your own, with a friend, or with a group, make the commitment to attend and be involved. You'll get the most out of this study if you commit to it. The curriculum is not overwhelming, so there are no excuses!

DISCUSSION

When talking in a group, be concise with your answers. Remember that everyone's time is precious, and everyone should have an opportunity to speak. What happens in the group, stays in the group. Keep discussion confidential. Scripture is our basis for everything. We may be drawn to giving worldly advice, but the best truth is God's!

If you are leading a group, see more tips for leaders at the end of this book in the Leader Guide.

WHY ABUNDANCE?

Moms are used to things in abundance—laundry, dishes, back talk, coffee. But abundant life? It seems like a far stretch, especially for moms, doesn't it? So, why is abundance important?

We all want more out of this life. We want a full, happy, joyful life—but the days run together and our fuses run short and our Bibles get dusty and we find ourselves further and further from abundance.

When we become moms, we are told that motherhood is all about "survival mode," and many of us believe that. Whether you are a brand-new mom—rocking your first baby, grasping the pages of this book, aching for a bit of hope—or your kids are grown and you're looking back, wanting to still be a mom of abundance for them in this stage, this study is for you.

Because we are tired of giving in to survival mode.

We are tired of letting the world tell us what we should be and where we should place our hope.

We are tired of letting fear and shame take the wheel.

We are tired of being less than what we were created to be.

Most of us are just tired.

But there is hope. And this hope is for you too, Mama. As you chase your toddler or rush your teenager off to football practice. As you tuck your children in and pray for them each night. It's our hope that you find abundance there—in those quiet (or not-so-quiet) and unseen moments, moments that aren't celebrated or splattered across social media. It's in those moments when we cry out to God and run toward abundance and leave behind survival mode, the expectations of the world, or the pressure we place on ourselves. It's there we find that all that matters are Jesus and this beautifully abundant life He offers us in Him. And we discover *abundance is for us all*.

And we won't sugarcoat it—motherhood is hard; we all know that. But it can be so much more. We can wake up every day and choose abundance. We can choose to say no to the tired, old life and choose to step into something new, fresh, and truly wonderful.

Will you run in abundance with us?

THE WAY IT WAS MEANT TO BE

It's not supposed to be like this. That sentence runs through my head more often than I'd like to admit as I survey my chaotic home, fighting children and my own short temper. Motherhood seemed so much more beautiful and easy from the outside looking in, but now, in the thick of it, many days I feel like I'm standing in quicksand.

Was it really supposed to be this way? Is it supposed to be this hard?

The short answer? No. It wasn't, and it's not.

Sin wrecked God's glorious plan for life with Him and flipped the script on what should be a full and abundant life, leaving us feeling shorthanded and grasping for a bit of hope. And if anything has taught me about falling short, hitting rock bottom, and finding grace again and again—it's parenting.

This week we are going to take a look back at God's original plan and where things all went wrong. I want us to think of this story as one of hope, not devastation. Where God could have given up when His creation turned against Him—He showed He was a God of second (and third and fourth and fifth) chances. Wouldn't you do the same for your child?

Although this may not be the way it was meant to be— God had a plan all along to lead us back to abundance with Him. So, hang with us, because there is good news, and there is hope.

Day One
BROKEN ABUNDANCE
Genesis 3:1-7

Crunch.

You know the feeling when you bite into a crisp, ripe fruit. It's a satisfying sound to your ears and an explosion on your taste buds. I imagine the sound when Eve took the bite of that forbidden fruit; it must have echoed through the garden of Eden. I'm sure the fruit in the garden was the juiciest and most delicious it's ever been in all of creation. The animals probably paused as the whole earth stood still in that world-shattering moment.

Before that infamous *crunch*, there was perfection. God had created this beautiful world. Everything was in order, working together perfectly. He put man and woman in the garden to live and create life together and to walk with Him. Man and woman and God lived together more intimately than we could ever imagine.

But before we go any further into this story—let's take a quick look at *abundance*. What is it?

Get out a dictionary (or, let's be honest—ask Siri or Alexa) and write down the meaning of *abundance*:

A very large quantity of Something.

What does *abundance* mean to you?

More than enough

Now, let's take a deeper look at where things all went wrong—the moment of broken abundance.

*✐ **Go to the Word:** Read Genesis 3:1-5 for the dialogue between the serpent and the woman.*

As we read in Genesis 3, the serpent (later in the Bible, in Revelation 12:9, referred to as the deceiver Satan) comes to the woman and tempts her: "Did God *really* say you can't eat from any tree?" (I imagine heavy sarcasm in his voice.) Eve responds, telling the serpent that they are allowed to eat from any tree but the tree in the middle of the garden, and if they do, they will die.

"You won't die!" the serpent responds to her.

You see—sin does this. It lies and manipulates. It tells us that it's okay. It promises something greater than we anticipated. It says whatever the cost of our disobedience is, it will all be worth it—but it never is.

What does sin do? lies + manipulates you. Makes you believe It doesnt matter when It matters alot.

In an instant, the perfect, beautiful bond between God and humankind was broken. The intimacy between God and human beings was made to be something really special. When we look back to the way it was intended to be, we know that God had this beautiful plan of perfect abundance in mind for them.

But when Eve believed the lies, she fell into the sin.

Go to the Word: *Read Genesis 3:6–7: "The woman saw that the tree was good for food and delightful to look at, and that it was desirable for obtaining wisdom. So she took some of its fruit and ate it; she also gave some to her husband, who was with her, and he ate it. Then the eyes of both of them were opened, and they knew they were naked; so they sewed fig leaves together and made coverings for themselves."*

When Adam and Eve first sinned, they felt shame. They realized their brokenness and wrongdoing, and their eyes were opened. They saw that they were naked and covered themselves. Sin brings shame, guilt, and brokenness. Sin is never worth the delicious *crunch*.

As hard as it may be to look back at our beginnings, there's good news—our story doesn't end here. Hope wasn't shattered that day. Abundance may have been broken, but God never leaves it that way. This is just the start of a truly beautiful story. It's important to revisit the story of the Fall to get a full picture of the way our relationship with God was meant to be and to grasp the significance of God's sacrifice, made for us so that we may have abundance with Him now.

What in your life promises to be worth it, but never is in the end? What lies is sin telling you today? These are the things that keep us from true abundance, and it's best to call them out now!

Overeating
Lashing out at the kids.
Gossiping.

Do you have stories of brokenness that are difficult to recall but have helped you on your path to following Jesus? Maybe you're in one of those stories right now. Sometimes it takes being broken and living in shame to lead us to a place of surrender. Write about one part of your story of brokenness.

Not being able to get pregnant broke me into a million pieces. I became angry and hated anyone that was happy with a baby.

Go to the Word: *The Bible is an entire work made up of many parts, all inspired by God and reflecting His plan. Read the following verses and write down what they tell you about God and His plan for His people.*

1 Peter 2:9–10

Romans 1:20

PRAYER FOR ABUNDANCE

Ask God to help you see what sins are holding you back from a life of abundance with Him. In the spaces provided after these prompts, write down any requests you make in prayer, and you can come back to review them later in the study.

Day Two

SEPARATION FROM GOD

Genesis 3:8–24

Consequences are something we learn about at a young age. You touch a hot stove; it burns you. You push your sister; she'll likely push back. You talk back to your mom; you might lose that movie-marathon weekend you've been planning. There were consequences for Adam and Eve when they chose to disobey God's instructions. And if anyone understands how much this must have broken God's heart, it's us moms. We beg our children to not do that *one* thing—but they almost always have to test their limits. Every time they cross that line, it breaks our hearts, because we want our children to trust us, and we want to save them from the consequences of disobedience. (Yeah, God, we hear You. We get the irony!)

What consequences have you had to deal with in your life because of disobedience?

*✍ **Go to the Word:** Read Genesis 3:8-13.*

We find Adam and Eve in Genesis 3, hunkered in the corner, knitting first-generation parachute pants and peasant tops (or whatever fashion trend they created), when God joins them in the garden. I find this to be one of the most fascinating parts of this story—chapter 3, verse 8—they "heard the sound of the LORD God walking in the garden at the time of the evening breeze." This paints a picture of the intimacy and relationship between this man and woman and God. The fact that God was moving around in the garden with them illustrates the way our relationship with God was meant to be. When I hear our back door click open and footsteps across our kitchen floor, I know my husband is home. We have a deep, intimate relationship, and I know exactly what he sounds like when he walks through the house. Adam and Eve knew the sound of God moving through the garden; they were that close!

God calls out to them, "Where are you?"

And Adam says, "I heard you coming, and I was afraid because I was naked, so I hid."

Okay, also a relatable scenario: 99.9 percent of the time, I'm excited when I hear my husband enter the house, but sometimes, when I haven't been the best wife, I feel the need to sneak away and hide from him. You know the feeling, right? (Sorry, honey, I haven't showered in three days, so I'm hiding in bed so you don't have to look at me!) Sometimes our first instinct when our behavior hasn't been ideal is to hide—even from those who love us the most.

God continues in verse 11 (with a question He already knows the answer to, because He's God, but He's driving the point home): "Who told you that you were naked? Did you eat from the tree that I commanded you not to eat from?"

As we keep reading, we see Adam and Eve play the blame game, and then eventually God hands down the consequences.

➤ **Go to the Word:** *Read Genesis 3:14–19. Pay attention to the consequences described for the serpent, woman, and man.*

Write down some of the consequences God gave to the man and woman.

The consequences given to Eve (in verse 16) are ones that many mothers understand well: the pains of bearing children and the struggles with marriage. While the childbirth part is pretty clear in this verse, the part about husbands can be a little more confusing. The statement of "he will rule over you" wasn't a biblical command for husbands to dominate wives, but can be understood better as a description of what was going to happen to the relationship between the two parties—that it would become problematic and complicated as opposed to the perfect partnership it had been. The battle of the sexes began!

How have you struggled with the same consequences given to Eve?

Go to the Word: Read Romans 1:18–25, and then answer the questions that follow. Look closely at verses 21–25:

> *For though they knew God, they did not glorify him as God or show gratitude. Instead,*

their thinking became worthless, and their senseless hearts were darkened. Claiming to be wise, they became fools and exchanged the glory of the immortal God for images resembling mortal man, birds, four-footed animals, and reptiles.

Therefore God delivered them over in the desires of their hearts to sexual impurity, so that their bodies were degraded among themselves. They exchanged the truth of God for a lie, and worshiped and served what has been created instead of the Creator, who is praised forever. Amen.

In Romans 1:18-25, how does Paul say that people have sinned against God? How does that sin separate us from God—what are the consequences we face?

▟ Go to the Word: Read Genesis 3:20-24.

While this story of Adam and Eve's disobedience has a solemn ending, it is sprinkled with a covering of hope. Before God sends them away and separates Himself from them, He pauses to make clothes for them (verse 21). It's a beautiful picture of grace—that God is constantly showing His love for His children even in the midst of utter heartbreak. He shows us this same grace each and every day, if we are willing to accept His offerings to us.

PRAYER FOR ABUNDANCE

Think about the consequences of your own sins and in what ways you have felt separated from God recently. Ask God to help you fully accept the grace that draws us close to Him.

Day Three

FAITHFUL OFFERINGS
Genesis 4:1–16

I had a very rose-colored view of parenting multiple children before I was in the midst of it. I assumed that, if I did everything right, my children would be the best of friends, always get along, and it would be smooth sailing. My husband and I had a great marriage (and still do), and I felt like we were building a pretty solid foundation for our kids. But I forgot about one thing—sin.

Sin was and is still part of the picture. It is for me, it is for you, and it was for Adam and Eve. My kids don't get along like I always dreamed they would, because there is sin in their hearts. Maybe from my Instagram page you would think they are the best of friends. And some days, well, in some *moments*, they are! But sin always creeps in and causes an uproar in our home.

As we continue to look at our first family in Genesis, we see Adam and Eve, having left the garden and been separated from God, go on to start populating the earth. Eve gives birth to two sons, Cain and Abel—and sin was there every step of the way. We don't see much of their childhood, but I'm sure that was interesting—without any of the "what to expect" books to help Eve out along the way. (The first time dealing with a toddler must have been a trip!)

We see the brothers grown up in Genesis 4, bringing offerings to the Lord. God finds favor with Abel and his offering but does not have regard for Cain and his offering.

✍ **Go to the Word:** *Look at Genesis 4:1–7. Verses 5–7 tell us: "Cain was furious, and he looked despondent. Then the*

LORD said to Cain, 'Why are you furious? And why do you look despondent? If you do what is right, won't you be accepted? But if you do not do what is right, sin is crouching at the door. Its desire is for you, but you must rule over it.'"

What did Cain offer God?

What did Abel offer?

Why did God not accept Cain's offering?

Cain, Cain, Cain. Resentful, jealous, entitled Cain. Scripture warns us in Jude 1:11 of people who went the "way of Cain"—worshipping God with impure motives. Cain brought his offering to the Lord with an impure heart. He offered something, but without a faithful and obedient heart, his offering meant nothing to the Lord.

Those who went the way of Cain were described by Jude as ungodly people who defiled themselves and rejected authority—they blasphemed "anything they do not understand" (verse 10). They were also "discontented grumblers, living according to their desires; their mouths utter arrogant words, flattering people for their own advantage" (verse 16). In general, they were people who might show up for worship or hang out with believers, but they would be there for all the wrong reasons.

In what ways have you ever gone the "way of Cain"?

~✐~ Go to the Word: Read Genesis 4:8-12.

Cain just can't take it anymore. The anger, envy, and sin in his heart are just too much. He lures his brother out to a field and murders him. (Did you learn nothing from your parents' mistakes, Cain?)

When sin entered the world, it led to a downhill spiral from generation to generation. Unfortunately, it wasn't a onetime mistake that Adam and Eve made—sin is a disease that infested the entire world and ruined the lives of their children as well.

What can you learn from this story about faithful offerings to God?

What do your offerings look like? Are you going to God with your own agenda, or is your heart set on worshipping Him?

PRAYER FOR ABUNDANCE

Consider what you've offered to God in the past few weeks or months—have you been giving Him the best of you? Ask God to open up your heart to gratitude. Sing a song or write out a psalm of thankfulness as a prayer.

Day Four

A CHOICE OF ABUNDANCE

John 10:7–10

Adam and Eve had a choice. Cain had a choice. We have choices we face every day—choices that either lead us deeper into abundance with God or lead us into sin that separates us from Him. And if we're honest, we like having choices in life; it makes us feel as though we are in the driver's seat. I give my children choices every day, hoping they will make the right ones and grow into responsible and smart human beings. God gives us the opportunities to make the right choices to lead us closer to Him as well.

We can choose sin (separation from God), or we can choose to devotedly follow God. We can choose to be pushed around by our impulses, or we can choose to live a life of purpose. We can choose survival mode, or we can choose abundant life.

Go to the Word: *In John 10:7–10, Jesus describes how He has come to bring us abundance:*

> *Truly I tell you, I am the gate for the sheep. All who came before me are thieves and robbers, but the sheep didn't listen to them. I am the gate. If anyone enters by me, he will be saved and will come in and go out and find pasture. A thief comes only to steal and kill and destroy. **I have come so that they may have life and have it in abundance.***

Write out the second half of John 10:10 in your own words.

What do you think this type of abundance looks like for your life?

In this passage, the thief who comes "to steal and kill and destroy" refers to false teachers. During Jesus' day, many false prophets claimed to be the way to God and the way to heaven. While the world has changed since biblical times, we still have plenty of false teachers, although they look a little different. Today's false teachers often preach a form of "feel good" Christianity and an "I can do it myself" mentality. We live in a world that wants us to believe we don't need God to be happy and full.[1]

What are some things that are "thieves" in your life? What things or people provide false promises of peace, purpose, and freedom?

Go to the Word: *We have a life offered to us that is better than we could have ever imagined; it's ours for the taking! Look up these scriptures and write down what the promises are for us in abundant life.*

Ephesians 3:20

2 Corinthians 5:17

Matthew 6:33

Psalm 16:11

Galatians 2:20

Luke 6:38

Far too often we get so caught up in survival mode that we forget abundant life is right in front of us to take for our own. Below is a simple comparison between survival mode and the abundant life that Jesus offers us:

Survival Mode	vs.	The Abundant Life
No time for God in your schedule	vs.	Desiring time with God ("But whoever drinks from the water that I will give him will never get thirsty again"—John 4:14)
Never stopping	vs.	Rest ("Therefore, since the promise to enter his rest remains, let us beware that none of you be found to have fallen short"—Hebrews 4:1)
Bitterness and comparison	vs.	Love ("We love because he first loved us"—1 John 4:19)
Sadness and depression	vs.	Joy ("I have told you these things so that my joy may be in you and your joy may be complete"—John 15:11)
Anxiety and worry for the future	vs.	Hope ("Rest in God alone, my soul, for my hope comes from him"—Psalm 62:5)
Boredom and restlessness	vs.	Mental and spiritual alertness of the battles around you ("Be sober-minded, be alert. Your adversary the devil is prowling around like a roaring lion, looking for anyone he can devour"—1 Peter 5:8)
Poor judgment and decision making	vs.	Wisdom ("For who has known the Lord's mind, that he may instruct him? But we have the mind of Christ"—1 Corinthians 2:16)
Following cultural or worldly standards	vs.	Not conforming to this world ("Because everyone who has been born of God conquers the world. This is the victory that has conquered the world: our faith"—1 John 5:4)
Selfishness	vs.	Compassion ("Just as you want others to do for you, do the same for them"—Luke 6:31)

Make your own list: What are the lies that you hear in survival mode? According to the scriptures we've looked at this week, what does abundance promise?

Survival Mode Says	Abundance Promises

Today, you have a choice to make. Will you choose survival mode? Or will you choose abundant life? When we make the choice for abundance over sin and survival, we are choosing to experience joy, peace, and rich and full life far greater than we could ever imagine!

PRAYER FOR ABUNDANCE

Think about the times this past week when you have been just surviving. Ask God to help you find purpose, peace, and hope even in the most overwhelming moments.

WEEK ONE

Group Discussion

STARTER

Begin by sharing with your group some stories from your week of mom life. What tasks have you had to do in abundance this past week? (Laundry? Dishes? Changing diapers? Math homework? Helping with college application forms?)

REVIEW

1. Give your definitions of the following words. You can share what you thought about these terms before you began the study. Have your ideas about these terms changed any?

    Abundance **is**

    Sin **is**

2. What did you learn about God's character through the study of the relationship of Adam and Eve and God?

3. How has sin put distance between you and God, hurting your abundance? (Note: Sin isn't always an easy thing to talk about in a group setting, but it is important to

confess our sins! Find a friend or mentor you are comfortable talking with if you feel uneasy about sharing specific sins in this group.)

4. How does survival mode lie to you in your daily life? What does abundance promise? (Look back to day four to get a refresher, and share what you wrote down.)

5. What is something you can change right now to help move you closer to walking in abundance? Focus on things you have control over—not on situations or behaviors of others that you can't change.

PRAYER FOR ABUNDANCE

Close your group time by hearing about the needs and desires of the group members. Pray for one another, asking God to help you see past survival mode and to reach for something better—abundant life with Him!

LIVING IN THE PAST

Our past tells who we are and where we came from—our stories. It even plays a role in shaping our futures. These all sound like positive things, yes? So why is it that when people talk about living in the past, it's not supposed to be a good thing?

Living in the past denotes being stuck or stagnant. You can't move forward when you are too absorbed with what has already taken place. So, although the past may hold many beautiful and sentimental memories, it can also significantly trip us up.

I'm sure you've seen or heard of movies that depict the washed-up former high school quarterback, twenty years older, still reminiscing about the state championship and the glory days. Those poor guys are never viewed as the heroes of their stories. Instead, they are sad, grown-up versions of their high school selves—never making anything of their lives. They are probably chasing girls a couple of decades younger than them. They have no real relationships. No accomplishments. Nothing to show for themselves.

While learning from the past is highly valuable, we need to know how to glean wisdom from a situation and then move forward. How can we experience abundance when we are unable to move on to bigger and better things? This week we focus on leaving the past behind us and stepping boldly into the future God has for us!

Day One

A NEW CREATION

Galatians 2:20–21; 2 Corinthians 5:17–18

Moms often remember the first cry of their newborns or the first time they looked into the eyes of their children. We spend many minutes marveling at the wonder of God's ability to form these little beings in the womb. In the same way the physical act of creation brings about new life, our spiritual birth and acceptance of Jesus' forgiveness results in new life. We are reborn and given a new identity in Him. We are made blameless and pure, like a sweet-smelling, newborn babe.

Go to the Word: Galatians 2:20–21 says, "I have been crucified with Christ, and I no longer live, but Christ lives in me. The life I now live in the body, I live by faith in the Son of God, who loved me and gave himself for me. I do not set aside the grace of God, for if righteousness comes through the law, then Christ died for nothing."

Look back at the passage and circle all the ways we are changed when we become a new creation in Christ.

We are crucified with Christ and He lives in us! That is a big deal! Being crucified with Christ is simply (and not so simply) the idea that the old self dies, just as Jesus died on the cross. And then, as Jesus rose again to life, we are forgiven and given the gracious gift of new life in Him! The thought of this opportunity for renewal is like a cool drink of water for my soul. What's it like for you?

Even though we have this new life, we often find ourselves fixated on our old selves. Our past sins haunt us. We worry about things we said in anger, lies we told—the list of wrongs goes on and on. But we have to remember, these are actions of our old selves. We no longer have to be defined or limited by the sin in our lives. We are free from shame and the fear of eternal punishment. The old self is dead. We can do something completely new.

Go to the Word: *2 Corinthians 5:17–18 says, "Therefore, if anyone is in Christ, he is a new creation; the old has passed away, and see, the new has come! Everything is from God, who has reconciled us to himself through Christ and has given us the ministry of reconciliation."*

In what ways are you continuing to dwell on who you *were* rather than who you *are* now in Christ? How might this fixation on the past be hindering you today?

We have to fix our eyes on the One who made us that new creation. He knows every aspect of our being. He understands our human tendencies. He walked here on earth just as we do. Seeking His plan for our lives will propel us forward into the glorious future He has for us.

Take a moment and think about what you need to release to the Father. Now imagine you are walking to the foot of the cross. Drop that heavy load and walk away. Feel the weight of your past burdens fall to the ground. How does it feel to lighten that load?

You can stand upright with your eyes fixed forward. Take a deep breath of relief and walk on. Don't turn and look back! You have given the rubbish that has so long weighed you down to the One who forgives, the One who restores, and the One who redeems! He has victory over all our past junk, and we are no longer defined by those things, but given new life and new direction! We are new creations, friend!

PRAYER FOR ABUNDANCE

Write down a few of the things that you need to leave at the cross of Christ—these could be past sins that still present temptations for you, or the shame of mistakes you made in the past that you have allowed to shape how you look at yourself, or something else. Ask Jesus to free you from being stuck in these past patterns and thoughts.

Day Two
LONGING FOR EGYPT
Exodus 16:1–5

"Mom! I want a cup of water!" "Mom, I need a snack!" "Mom, Mom, MOM!" Do you ever wonder if being God feels a lot like being a mom? Always hearing demands and hardly ever receiving thanks? Honestly, my kids sometimes ask for a snack in a tone that would make a passing stranger think they never get fed!

Many times, we demand that God fulfill our "needs," and we plead as though we have to convince Him to care for us, instead of trusting Him to provide for us. We are not so different from how the Israelites were thousands of years ago. We see an example of this in Exodus. The Israelites have been freed from bondage in Egypt, but when the rubber hits the road, their faith falters.

Go to the Word: *Read Exodus 16:1–5. Focus on verse 3: "The Israelites said to them, 'If only we had died by the LORD's hand in the land of Egypt, when we sat by pots of meat and ate all the bread we wanted. Instead, you brought us into this wilderness to make this whole assembly die of hunger!'"*

Oh, those Israelites and their flip-flop faith! If you have spent any time reading in Exodus or seen any movies about Moses' life, you have no doubt run across at least one story of the Israelites' lack of conviction. Even after God gives them reason after reason to trust in His provision, they fall prey to insecurity and doubt. The Lord promised them an abundant life, but they were unable to see past their hunger pains.

➷ Go to the Word: *Look at the verses listed below and note all the ways the Lord showed His faithfulness to the Israelites in the wilderness.*

Exodus 14:5–31

Exodus 15:22–27

Exodus 16:11–19

Exodus 17:1–7

Time and time again, the Israelites complained and grumbled. They even asked to go back to Egypt rather than continue on to the Promised Land. They had zero perspective on the past. They chose to remember only the things they wanted to remember instead of weighing the true nature of their situation and trusting in the Lord to provide. Back in Egypt, they had been slaves with no freedom for crying out loud! I don't know about you, but I would certainly choose freedom over bondage!

Have you ever had a moment when living in the past seemed like it would be better than dealing with your current troubles? What made you feel that way?

Just like the Israelites, we are limited human beings. We cannot know the fullness of the future. We are trapped in a continuing moment that seamlessly ebbs and flows into the next, in an unending sequence of events. When we are in the midst of difficult situations, it can be hard to see past what's right in front of us. Once those moments pass, they are just that: the past. We cannot change the past, but we can learn from it and look toward the future.

If the Israelites had kept the proper perspective, they would have remembered the promises God had made to them. They would have imagined the land flowing with milk and honey. They would have seen the bountiful life awaiting them.

Recall a time in your life when you were in the middle of a difficult situation, and you struggled to trust that the Lord would come through for you, but in the end, He showed Himself faithful. Write or draw something that reminds you of that time.

Now think of a time when you were again in a difficult situation, but you were able to keep perspective and trust the Lord because He had shown Himself faithful to you in the past. What was different about that time?

Thank goodness we have a gracious God who understands what it means to be human. His grace and mercy for us know no bounds. Like the Israelites, we constantly doubt His goodness and try to take matters into our own hands. But He is patient with us. And He leads us faithfully into the future.

PRAYER FOR ABUNDANCE

Spend some time with the Father now. Share with Him any doubts you may be struggling with, or a situation you need guidance in. He wants to give to us abundantly; we just need to trust Him to keep His promises. Thankfully, we serve a God who can be trusted.

Day Three

FROM BLESSINGS TO BITTERNESS AND BACK AGAIN
Ruth 1–2

About five years ago, I was feeling overwhelmed. I was quite pregnant with our second child, and our list of needs was steadily growing—a house to rent, more income, another crib. On and on, the list grew. I am a list maker by nature, so when needs are piling up, I tend to grab pen and paper to help settle my nerves. I wrote down all the things I could think of that were weighing on my mind—all the things that we needed but felt unattainable. I then folded my list into a small square and slid it into a little envelope taped inside the back cover of my Bible.

Laying my hands over the envelope, I prayed to the Lord. I thanked Him for being our provider and for being a trustworthy God. I asked Him to help me trust His provision and forget about the things written on the list. And I did forget.

A few months passed, and during my devotions one day I stumbled across the list. Having forgotten about it, I was curious to read the things I had written down only a few months prior. I was amazed to see that almost every item on that list could now be checked off. Seeing the Lord's provision in such a tangible way was a glorious reminder of His desire to create abundance in our lives!

Today, we will take a look at the story of Ruth and Naomi, two women brought together through family relationships and some tragic circumstances. We will see how an overwhelmed Naomi experienced that the Lord was faithful to create abundance out of chaos.

⌒z⌒ **Go to the Word:** *Read Ruth 1:1–5.*

Let's look at this story to gain some context. The Israelite man Elimelech and his wife, Naomi, rather than trusting the Lord to get them through a difficult time, picked up and left Bethlehem for the land of Moab. (The Moabites were descendants of Lot and his daughter through incest. Not a great way to start a tribe!) They went somewhere they shouldn't in an attempt to flee the famine in their own land. They became foreigners in a land full of those thought by the Jews (the Israelites) to be unclean. The Moabites worshipped other gods instead of the one true God.

We don't know all the details, but it would seem that Elimelech's family abandoned the land of their ancestors. Their choices were governed by fear, and they weren't trusting in the Lord. They left the land of their inheritance, and their sons took foreign wives in a strange land.

Can you recall a time when you attempted to solve a problem with your own power and on your own schedule rather than trusting the Lord? How did that play out?

⌒z⌒ **Go to the Word:** *Read Ruth 1:6–17.*

Imagine you are Naomi, living in a land you still feel is foreign. And then all the men around you who gave you security and safety have died, one by one. What would

you do? Would you be able to trust God in that situation? What do you think?

After the death of her husband and sons, Naomi gave up on the plan to live in Moab, even though she had been there now for more than a decade. She heard there might finally be food again back home, so she sent her daughters-in-law away to go back to their Moabite families. She described her life as "too bitter for you to share" (verse 13), and she felt that the Lord had turned against her. For Naomi, it seemed any chance of happiness was gone. She now was just focused on survival.

Obedient Orpah, after protesting, left her mother-in-law. But Ruth promised to stay until death should part them, pledging to Naomi that "wherever you go, I will go, and wherever you live, I will live; your people will be my people, and your God will be my God" (verse 16).

Naomi left the past behind and headed back to Bethlehem, her hometown, to start anew. Where else could she go? Often when we find ourselves in life-altering situations, we do one of two things—either we remain frozen with fear and doubt and choose not to move forward, or we trust in what we cannot see and continue on in faith.

 Go to the Word: *Read Ruth 1:18–22; 2:1–23.*

Even though Naomi felt God was against her, she and Ruth decided to depend on the provision of the Lord. They entered

Bethlehem and tried to live a normal life. But Naomi was still so bitter, she asked people to call her "Mara," meaning "bitter."

Ruth, however, was not bitter. She found work to do and went at it, determined to take care of her mother-in-law. She kept moving forward, fully embracing this new abundant life and depending on God.

But this life was not easy. The Lord had made provisions in the Law for widows, orphans, and the poor, but they still had to work hard. Naomi knew that, according to the Law, at harvest farmers were to leave the corners of their fields untouched to allow the poor and hungry to pick and eat (Leviticus 19:9). So she sent Ruth out to gather grain.

➛ **Go to the Word:** *Read Deuteronomy 24:19–21 and note all the ways the Lord makes provisions for those in need:*

> *When you reap the harvest in your field, and you forget a sheaf in the field, do not go back to get it. It is to be left for the resident alien, the fatherless, and the widow, so that the LORD your God may bless you in all the work of your hands. When you knock down the fruit from your olive tree, do not go over the branches again. What remains will be for the resident alien, the fatherless, and the widow. When you gather the grapes of your vineyard, do not glean what is left. What remains will be for the resident alien, the fatherless, and the widow.*

Ruth went and gleaned according to what she was supposed to do and what the Law allowed. She did not know everything about the faith of the Jews, but she trusted what Naomi had taught her and she trusted Naomi's God. And so the Lord brought her to the field belonging to Boaz, an important and good man who was also a relative of Elimelech, Naomi's late husband.

Who has the Lord given you to mentor and guide you? How has this person spoken truth into your life?

If you don't have a mentor in your life, consider finding someone (maybe even someone in the group, if you are participating in a group Bible study) who has been walking out their faith for longer than you have. In what areas of your life right now could you benefit from some faithful guidance?

Ruth and Boaz eventually married (see Ruth 4:1–13), and Naomi transformed from a blues singer to a ringleader of praise. People around her saw what the Lord had done for her and her family. She now had grandchildren and was cared for by a provider, Boaz. Ruth, the Moabite, was now praised by the Jews as "better to you than seven sons" (4:15) and was recognized for her love and care of Naomi. And from Ruth came a "family redeemer" to "renew your life and sustain you" (verses 14–15)—her son Obed, who then became the grandfather of King David, from whose family line would one day come the Redeemer of the world—Jesus.

What a blessing! This life of abundance began with a story of heartache and loss. The abundance came through God's provision and through hard work and determination. The abundance came from many steps of faith and hope. This abundance that Naomi and Ruth experienced came because the Lord remained faithful to His promises to Israel to bless those who seek Him and keep His Law.

PRAYER FOR ABUNDANCE

Think about examples of abundance you have experienced through trusting the Lord to provide and through trusting in following His commands. Thank God for all He has provided for you and your family.

Day Four

LEAVING THE PAST IN THE PAST
Philippians 3:13–14

Paul wasn't always Paul. Before Paul was the apostle that he is now remembered to be, he was Saul—Saul from the city of Tarsus. He grew up in a devout home and was zealous in his Jewish faith and traditions (Philippians 3:4–6). He was mentored by the greatest teacher of his day, Gamaliel (Acts 22:3), and joined the most influential sect of Judaism in his day, the Pharisees.

*➤ **Go to the Word:** Read Philippians 3:4–6.*

What are all the boasts in the list that Paul gives?

Saul became Paul after meeting Jesus. His very name was left behind, as was his misplaced zeal. Instead of being willing to kill for what he thought was God's will, Paul would die for his God through the humility that Jesus' life would teach him (Philippians 1:21).

Do you think that Paul was ever haunted by the actions he took before he came to Christ? He was human; therefore, I'd venture to say yes, probably so.

◢▱ ***Go to the Word:*** *Read the verses below to get an idea of how Paul describes himself in light of his sin. Write out Paul's descriptions.*

1 Corinthians 15:9

Ephesians 3:8

1 Timothy 1:15

Notice also that these three references are given in chronological order. Paul's view of himself does not improve over time; in fact, it lessens! Just like John writes (John 3:30), Paul becomes less, so that Christ may become more! Paul's view of himself in light of his sin is a humble one. He recognizes that God is greater—greater than him, greater than his past sin, or even his future transgressions. He has proper perspective but doesn't lose hope for the future (Philippians 3:12–14). His view of the past spurs him on toward that which is to come. And in Romans 8, Paul gives encouragement to the believers.

◢▱ ***Go to the Word:*** *Read Romans 8.*

List a few encouragements that speak to your heart.

Why is the recognition of our sin so very important?

Think about it like this: if we aren't really "THAT bad," then grace isn't really THAT good. The sobering reality is that we are all dirty, rotten sinners. Our culture today wants to tell us that we are perfect just the way we are and that no one should try to change us! I'm sorry, friend, but that is quite simply a lie. We are the farthest thing from perfect!

Unlike the world we live in, where many feel threatened by this truth, we serve a God who redeems! His power is made perfect in our weakness (2 Corinthians 12:9). He has made us a part of His powerful story of redemption. We get to play a role in the furthering of His kingdom. We are not just the powerless being saved by the powerful. We have been given the power of the Holy Spirit! How's that for empowerment for you?!

When we are remembering who we were before we knew Jesus, it is good to keep our current position *in* Jesus in view. In the chart below, explore what the verses state about our status before and after Jesus.

What was true about us without Jesus?		What does Jesus say about His followers?	
Romans 6:12	Sin reigns in our bodies.	Romans 6:6	No longer a slave to sin.
Psalm 51:5	Born in sin.	John 15:15	We are friends of Jesus.
James 2:10	If we fail in one point, account-able for the whole of the Law.	1 Corinthians 6:19	Our bod-ies are the temples of the Holy Spirit.
Romans 3:23	All have sinned. All have fallen short of the glory of God.	Ephesians 1:3	Blessed with every spiritual blessing in the heavenly realms.
Ecclesiastes 7:20	There is not a righteous person on earth who does not sin.	2 Corinthians 5:21	We can become the righteous-ness of God.

No matter what we've done or where we've come from, each of us has a part to play in the health and growth of the body of Christ. What role do you feel called to fill as a member of that body?

What types of abilities or spiritual gifts (check out Romans 12) has God given you?

How do you think the Lord could use you if you let Him?

➤ **Go to the Word:** *Read Hebrews 12:1 (NIV):*

> *Therefore, since we are surrounded by such a great cloud of witnesses,* **let us throw off everything that hinders and the sin that so easily entangles.** *And let us run with perseverance the race marked out for us.*

The writer of Hebrews is giving us permission to throw off those past sins, shame, or whatever burdens we carry, and just run. Sometimes we feel guilty about moving forward when there is sin in our past, but the Lord wants us to actually run this race.

PRAYER FOR ABUNDANCE

If you are still dealing with consequences from wrongs in your past, ask God for the wisdom to learn from those issues, the strength to move past them, and the faith to believe in the plan He has for you.

Group Discussion

STARTER

Begin by sharing some stories from your past. Tell one story from your younger years that is "on brand"—in other words, it is something that very much reflects who you are today.

REVIEW

1. Talk about when you first accepted Christ as your Savior. How have you been changed by living with Christ in you? If you haven't experienced that yet, what do you think is holding you back?

2. In this week's study, we've been thinking a lot about what it means to be a new creation. What does that mean to you? How do you feel like Christ has made you new?

3. Are there circumstances in your life right now that are causing you to doubt the Lord's goodness? Perhaps you

are persevering in the midst of a trial. How is the Lord speaking to you through this?

4. How has the Lord provided for you in the past (physically, emotionally, spiritually)? What has that revealed to you about His character?

5. Is there sin in your life now or shame from sins in the past that hinders you from living in the full abundance of Christ? What are some practical steps you can take this week to move past those things so you can run the race God has set out for you?

PRAYER FOR ABUNDANCE

Dealing with what is in our past may not be easy and it sometimes takes a long time. Remembering what God has done for us in the past can also be hard to do—especially in those weeks when we struggle to remember our children's names. As you pray for one another this week, have each person briefly name out loud one good thing God has done for them. For example, a person might say "Forgiveness," "Made my sister well," "Gave me hope," "Helped me get through divorce," "Gave me a friend," etc. After each person has had a chance to name something, let someone close the prayer time by thanking God for all of His good gifts to us in the past, and to help us remember what He has done for us every day this week.

Room to Reflect

TIME ISN'T ALWAYS ON OUR SIDE

Have you been waiting for God to give you something? A perfect husband? Another child? The perfect house? A promotion or raise? Maybe just a little recognition for the eight loads of laundry you did yesterday? You have been waiting and waiting, and you feel like it should be your time and that you deserve whatever blessing God should be giving you. *Right?*

I think we've all been there. But God's timeline is not our timeline. He works in His own way, and as Scripture says, He is working all things together for our good.

According to God's timeline, old age was the perfect time for Abraham and Sarah to finally have a baby, Lazarus was to be healed only after his death, and Jesus should spend thirty years on earth to do just three years of ministry. Sometimes God's timing and plans don't make sense to us, but they always make sense to God.

This week we are going to look a little closer at the difference between God's time and ours, deep-dive into the story of Abraham and Sarah, and wrap up with what we can learn from the example Jesus set for us in waiting on the Lord. We must remember to keep our eyes set on Jesus and keep running daily in abundance, knowing that God is setting our course. Jesus is the same yesterday, today, and forever (Hebrews 13:8), so even when the waiting gets hard or the timing doesn't feel right, we can remember that God is in control, and He's unwavering in His plan and love for us.

Day One

A TIME UNLIKE OURS

Joshua 1–3

My three-year-old can't tell time. Yet he continuously asks me what time it is, as if it has some sort of bearing on his world: "Mama, what time is it?" Ten times a day he asks me, and I glance at my watch to give him the time, even though I know this means nothing to him.

In our Western culture, time is of the essence. We are always on a strict schedule, running from place to place. We are bound to our timelines. So, why are we surprised when our children become obsessed with time?

We must assume that God works on the same type of schedule. We are constantly bringing up this issue with God, with one foot tapping angrily and frequent glances at our watches:

"Do you know what time it is?"

"Don't you know this should have happened by now, Lord?"

"God, when are You going to answer me?"

We are expecting Him to come through on our timeline. But God works in a time unlike ours. God is a God of opportunity, working outside of time. I love the way authors E. Randolph Richards and Brandon J. O'Brien explain this misunderstanding of time: "Biblical authors, like many non-Westerners, were less concerned with clock or calendar time (*chronos*) and more concerned with the appropriateness and fittingness of events (*kairos*). You might say they were more concerned with *timing* than with time."[1]

Look up the words below in a Greek dictionary or online and write down what these terms for *time* mean:

Chronos

Kairos

Timing is important, especially in Western culture, and I believe even more so for women and moms. We have a lot of things to keep in line and organized. Timing to us is *chronos*. It's a timeline of order, of chronology, of sequence. But timing to God is *kairos*. It's about a season, a window of opportunity, a proper time for proper action. While we may have a timeline for when we *want* things to happen, God always knows when it is *best* for things to happen.

Take, for instance, the Israelites as they were about to enter the Promised Land. They camped near the bank of the Jordan River, waiting to enter Canaan. There they faced a reminder that I think we all face at some point in our lives—that God's timing is very unlike our own. When the spies returned from Jericho, Joshua received the long-awaited news: "The LORD has handed over the entire land to us" (Joshua 2:24).

Go to the Word: *Read Joshua 1–3.*

What did God have the people do instead of letting them go straight into the Promised Land?

The extremely long journey to the Promised Land is cut short of the goal! We can imagine that, after generations of waiting, the Israelites were thrilled that their time (*chronos*) had finally arrived. But God used this opportunity (*kairos*) to drive home the lesson of faithfulness in their waiting. God desires that we respond faithfully in times of waiting and that we look to Him for the best opportunities, instead of being locked into our own timelines. Changing our focus in this way helps to shift our mind-set toward abundance. We never know what Promised Land might be right across the rushing waters, just a few days ahead of us!

In what current situation do you need to focus on the *kairos* (God's timing, and opportunities to see Him working) rather than the *chronos* (your own idea of when things need to be done)?

How does shifting your mind-set from *chronos* to *kairos* help you live in abundance?

PRAYER FOR ABUNDANCE

Ask God to help you see more clearly opportunities to join Him in His work, and ask Him for patience to make it through those times when you don't understand His plan.

Day Two
THE CALL OF ABRAM
Genesis 12–15

We had a deal, God. You aren't following through with Your end of the promise. Have you ever had this thought? I have. Often. I am a planner, and I like things to run on my schedule and on my time. As I pore over my planner each week to keep my four kids and our insanity of school, activities, church, and life in general in some sort of order, I continue to ask God, "Why are there still things I'm waiting on here?"

But, guys, I have news for you (especially for the type-A women out there): GOD DOES NOT USE A PLANNER. He doesn't pull out His set of pretty pens and highlighters and have everything penciled in for the week. He has a big and wonderful plan, but as we learned yesterday—*His time does not work like ours.*

That is a truth that is constantly hard for me to wrap my mind around—especially during the six years it took for us to finally adopt a child instead of the one or two years I had planned on, or when my husband spent a year unemployed while we had two young children. We aren't alone. Abram—the man considered the father of the Israelites, the man God spoke to directly—struggled with this fact as well. In Genesis 12, we read about God calling Abram.

✎ **Go to the Word:** *Read Genesis 12:1–3:*

> The Lord said to Abram:
>
> Go out from your land,
> your relatives,

and your father's house
to the land that I will show you.
I will make you into a great nation,
I will bless you,
I will make your name great,
and you will be a blessing.
I will bless those who bless you,
I will curse anyone who treats you with
    contempt,
and all the peoples on earth
will be blessed through you.

What did God tell Abram to do specifically?

List the seven things God promised Abram.

Now look at the verses again. Is Abram given a timeline or a deadline by which all these things should be accomplished? Read on to verse 4. How old was Abram when this promise was given?

Write down a promise you think God has given you that hasn't been fulfilled—and that you may feel frustrated about.

Go to the Word: Read through Genesis 12–15 and trace Abram's journey. (Today's reading is lengthy but important for understanding the story of Abram and God's promises to him.)

Write down your own brief summary of what happened after Abram set out from Haran up until the time God made a covenant with him (in chapter 15).

After Abram left Haran, we see a time when he seemed to lack trust in God's plan and took matters into his own hands. What happened? What were the costs of his plans?

How do you rationalize your own turning away from God's directions?

What has your disobedience to God or lack of trust in His leading cost you or others in your life?

As we learned in week one, God's plan was always for abundant life with His creation. It was our sin that separated us from Him and divided us from abundance. God also longed to give abundance to Abram; He wasn't out to trip him up or punish him! God made promises to Abram, and God's promises are always fulfilled. We just don't always understand God's timing, so we feel like we need to set the path for God to follow. When God calls us to step out in faith, He requires us to trust Him every step of the way.

Even when Abram (more on that name tomorrow!) faced times of uncertainty and questioned God's plan, he kept his faith that God's promises would be fulfilled. And they were.

PRAYER FOR ABUNDANCE

Trust takes time and practice. Even though we have every reason to trust that God knows what is best for us, we still have a hard time surrendering our planners to Him. Ask God to help you practice trusting Him this week, in every minute of every hour.

Day Three

NEW NAME, PROMISE REMAINS
Genesis 16–21

My husband and I began our adoption process in April of 2010. In February of 2016, we brought our adopted son home. This made no sense to us in the six years of waiting, changed plans, and frustrated timing. It may not have fit my timeline, but it fit God's; and it makes complete sense now, knowing all along we were waiting for that little boy He had handpicked for us.

✍ **Go to the Word:** *Read Genesis 16.*

Many years after God's promise to and calling of Abram, this man (who was supposed to be the father of countless descendants, remember?) and his wife, Sarai, still had not had *any* children (Genesis 16:1). So Sarai recommended that Abram go and have a child with their servant Hagar, thinking that maybe they could build a family through her. Abram agreed, and Hagar became pregnant with Abram's child, causing increased tension for everyone.

Write down the players in this story of Abram; how many people were involved? Consider how many lives were affected by Abram's lack of trust in God's timing.

Go to the Word: *Read through Genesis 16–18:15; 21:1–7.*
(Today's reading is lengthy but important for understanding
the story of Abram/Abraham, Sarai/Sarah, and the fulfillment
of God's promises to them.)

What do you learn about Sarah through these scriptures?

What are the results of Abraham and Sarah taking things into their own hands again? What can we learn from this?

In Genesis 17, we read that God appeared to Abram when he was ninety-nine years old. This is always significant to me when I consider the fact that God's timing is so different from our own—He can use us and change us at any time! And He can change us in ways we don't expect at all. God told Abram, "I am God Almighty. Live in my presence and be blameless. I will set up my covenant between me and you, and I will multiply you greatly" (verses 1–2). Then God changed Abram's name, then and there, to *Abraham*, which means "father of a multitude." This new name wasn't just a change of a few letters. It reflected the change in Abraham's life and purpose. It was a symbol of God's faithfulness in His covenant with this man and his descendants—God was going to make His promises come true.

Look up *covenant* in a dictionary and write the definition here.

The word for *covenant* in the Hebrew language is transliterated as *berith* and likely derives from another word meaning "to bind" or a "bond." As author Louis Berkhof states, "In the measure in which one of the parties is subordinate and has less to say, the covenant acquires the character of a disposition or arrangement imposed by one party on the other."[2] This reminds us that God and (the newly named) Abraham are not equal parties making negotiations and signing an agreement. God brings the covenant to the table on His terms, and Abraham is grateful to have a seat at the table.

Go to the Word: *Read through Genesis 17:3–16.*

17:3–8	"As for me …"	God's part of the covenant:
17:9–14	"As for you …"	Abraham's part of the covenant:

17:15-16	"As for Sarai ..."	The promise for Sarai:

Waiting can be hard, but God is always faithful, even when what He is doing doesn't line up with our timeline.

Go to the Word: Read through the verses presented below and trace Abraham's timeline.

Age of Abraham when God called him (Genesis 12:4) ____.

Age of Abraham when Sarah gave Hagar to him as his wife (16:3) _____.

Age of Abraham when Hagar bore Ishmael to him (16:16) ____.

Age of Abraham when God revisited him, changed his name, and established the covenant of circumcision (17:1-14) ____.

Age of Abraham when Isaac was born to him (21:5) ____.

These milestones in Abraham's life show us that something might not happen in the season we hope for or when we believe that it should (or even in our lifetime), but God's promises are always true.

When we look at Abraham and Sarah's story, it's easy to think, *Wow, they messed up so much, how could God have ever used them?* But if you have ever been to Sunday school, you will have heard Abraham's story as a source of learning about God's faithfulness and praising God for His provision, as heard in this children's song: "Father Abraham had many sons, and many sons had Father Abraham. I am one of them, and so are you, so let's just praise the Lord!"

Abraham may have stumbled, but he still trusted in the Lord, and God used him. In Hebrews 11, where we see the Hall of Fame of the great people of faith, we read of Abraham and Sarah's story of faith. We don't read of their mistakes, but of their obedience and trust in God.

✐ **Go to the Word:** *Read Romans 4:13-25.*

What does this scripture tell you about Abraham's faith?

How has God worked out impossible things in your life? Were you surprised by His timing?

No matter how many times we question the timing of God's promises, He is always right on time. He was for Abraham and Sarah—even when those promises seemed laughable. (I would laugh too—or maybe cry—if God told me I'd have a son at ninety!) God is right on time for us too.

PRAYER FOR ABUNDANCE

Take some time to think about promises God has given you through His Word. Thank God for the promises that you have seen fulfilled already.

Day Four

DOING THE IMPORTANT WORK
Matthew 8; Mark 5 and 10; Luke 19 and 24; John 4

We can look at story after story in Scripture to see God at work in His time (remember *kairos* and *chronos*?), outside of a timeline that makes sense to our human minds. You can sit in a room of people, and everyone can share a dozen stories about timing (*chronos*) that didn't make sense in the moment, but God intervened at the perfect opportunity (*kairos*), and it all came together so beautifully.

We can learn from these stories, but we can also learn from the life of Jesus. Jesus walked on this earth, existing in our time and space. He walked in our *chronos*, even as He was sent here out of God's perfect *kairos*. We can look to Jesus' life and study His example to understand how we should respond to God's plan.

There are different theories on exactly how long Jesus' earthly ministry lasted, but most scholars believe it was around three to three and a half years. This has always been fascinating to me, and has taught me so much about how God's timing is different from our own. We may have a "hustle and get it all done" mentality, but the Son of God came for thirty years before He even began traveling and ministering to people. You'd think that Jesus, being the Son of God, would supernaturally have the ability to do anything at any time (and He does), but He waited for the right opportunity (God's *kairos*!) before He set out on His ministry. It may not make sense to us, but it was exactly how God wanted it done. Let's settle in and learn from Jesus a bit today.

✐ **Go to the Word:** *Look up the following scriptures and note the difference between Jesus' reaction and the people's reaction to each situation.*

Matthew 8:1-4

Mark 5:25-34

Mark 10:17-27

Luke 19:1-10

Luke 24:13-39

John 4:7-26

Jesus noticed people. He listened. He touched. He saw. He never considered Himself too good, or too busy, to be available for someone—no matter who it was. Even if it didn't make sense to others, it always made sense to Him.

When you look at the way Jesus ministered to people, what do you think about how Jesus used His time?

What aspects of Jesus' schedule or His perspective on time would you like to add to your own life?

Jesus cared deeply for people. He stopped to care for anyone and everyone He came in contact with along His ministry. And while He did spend time caring for the sick, the poor, the hungry, and the broken, He also spent a lot of time pouring into His disciples—the small community who was always with Him. His family.

His disciples, who then went on to change the world (see the book of Acts), were the people whom God placed in His life for that time. That wasn't an accident, and they were definitely not a stumbling block to His work. Some might say the development of His disciples was one of the most important works He did on earth.

Let this be a reminder on the days when you are overwhelmed and exhausted by motherhood and the strains it puts on you. When you feel like you should be doing something bigger, something more important—remember Jesus and how He poured into the people around Him, even in the very limited time He had on earth to minister to them. The work of mothering could be the most important work you will ever do. It's worth every minute you spend on it.

Being a mom is not only one of the most important things you will ever do; it is spiritual work, it is holy work, and it is 100 percent God honoring. It is not just part of the work you will do in your life; it is *the* work.

Being a mom isn't something you do for eighteen years and then move on to make a difference in the world. The work you are doing right now, this ministry at your feet, is the good stuff. The wiping, the cleaning, the training up, the hugging, the encouraging. This is the work that changes the world. Whether you are a working mom, a foster mom, a stay-at-home mom, or a mom-in-waiting, you are right where you are supposed to be.[5]

Group Discussion

STARTER

Talk about your schedule this week. Did things go according to plan? Or not so much? Where did your ideal timing get messed up? (And which child was to blame?—just kidding ... maybe.)

REVIEW

1. Discuss the differences between *chronos* and *kairos*:
   Chronos

   Kairos

2. "God desires that we respond faithfully in times of waiting and that we look to Him for the best opportunities (*kairos*), instead of being locked into our own timelines (*chronos*). Changing our focus in this way helps to shift our mind-set toward abundance" (from day one). In what current situation do you need to leave your planner behind and focus on *kairos* rather than *chronos*? (You may want to look back to your answers from day one.)

3. In looking at Genesis 12, we learned that God made promises to Abram, but they weren't set on a timeline that made sense to him. When God calls us to step out in faith, He requires us to trust Him every step of the way. In what ways are you struggling to trust God with the timing of your circumstances?

4. Waiting on God's timing in our lives can be hard. Read Romans 4:13–25 as a reminder of Abraham's faith and God's promises. Share with the group a time when you were waiting on God's promises to be fulfilled (you might even be in one of those times now). Encourage one another to recognize and remember God's faithfulness.

5. Take some time to reflect together on the life of Jesus and the way He spent most of His time on earth. What about Jesus' life reminds you of the important work of mothering? What activities of His life or qualities of His schedule do you wish you had more of in your life?

PRAYER FOR ABUNDANCE

Use your prayer time as an experiment in waiting, having patience, and listening for God. Allow for two minutes of silent prayer, then invite members of the group to speak requests for help in understanding God's timing more and/or offer thanks for God's faithfulness. Everyone can speak when she is feeling led to speak. Let one person close the prayer after allowing time for people to speak.

Room to Reflect

DON'T LET FEAR STEAL YOUR ABUNDANCE

As mothers, fear is something we live with almost daily. In the little things and the big things, there are endless temptations to give in to fear. Fear for our children's physical safety, emotional well-being, health, interactions with others, behavior in public, keeping up at school—it's a long list. On top of that, we have fears about ourselves, spouses, friends, extended family, careers, accomplishments, and our homes.

Fear is a huge foothold for our enemy, Satan. If he can make us fearful, he can so easily take hold in many areas of our lives. How much more vulnerable are we when we are afraid? I'd say quite a lot.

The good news is, Jesus commands us in the Bible, "Fear not!" And this command doesn't come without instruction and direction. He doesn't say, "Fear not … now, good luck out there!" The Lord stands with us! Isaiah 41:10 says, "Do not fear, for I am with you; do not be afraid, for I am your God. I will strengthen you; I will help you; I will hold on to you with my righteous right hand."

That right there is a promise from the Lord God. He has our backs! This week, we look at four examples of fear in the Bible and learn how to trust God's promises more.

Day One

THE PARABLE OF THE TALENTS
Matthew 25:14–30

I am NOT a risk taker. I eat the same foods at restaurants, enjoy being at home, and hate conflict of any kind; you will never catch me jumping out of a plane. In all honesty, I am comfortable with being this way, but sometimes I find myself losing out as a result. In the smallest ways, I'm allowing fear to dictate my life. I don't order a dish I haven't tried for fear I won't like it, so instead I stick with the ol' chicken finger standby. Have you ever noticed, though, how often the Lord hands us a situation or opportunity that forces us to dive headlong into our fear?

When the parable of the talents is taught, people often focus on the servant who buries what was given to him because he was fearful. But consider this: What if all three servants were fearful, but only one allowed it to dictate his decisions? They were each given a ton of someone else's money to manage, and I'm willing to bet they were all pretty nervous about the outcome of their own actions. But only one chose to let his fear run the show.

↝ *Go to the Word:* *Read Matthew 25:14-18.*

A master was going on a long journey and gave five, two, and one talent(s) of gold to his three servants (more on what a talent is later). He gave to them "depending on each one's ability" (Matthew 25:15). This means it was not random. The master had the objective of receiving a return on his investment. In order to do this, he gave according to each servant's abilities. What abilities? Perhaps the master considered their wisdom, trustworthiness, economic savvy, and shrewdness in business practices of the day.

Before we go further, let's stop and answer the question of what exactly is a talent? A talent was a unit of weight in Bible times. Specifically in this story, it was a weight of money or value. Some scholars have said that a talent of gold was equal to 3,000 shekels, or 75 pounds of gold. Given the current price of gold at the time of writing this chapter, this amount of gold would come to about $1.5 million by today's standards.

Another way of looking at it is to consider the wages of laborers of the first century. According to Bible scholars, one talent would have been equal to the wages a worker could earn in twenty years. Twenty years!

Basically, it was a significant amount of money.

Go to the Word: Read Matthew 25:19–23.

What did the first two servants do with what the master had given them?

How are the two faithful servants rewarded?

Notice that, twice, the master invites the faithful servants to share or enter into their master's joy. Why do you think the master says this?

Not only are the faithful servants entrusted with more, but their reward is even more exceedingly abundant! They are given an invitation to share in their master's wealth! Joy is a stark contrast to fear—you really can't get further from it! The faithful servants are given more wealth and their _____ exchanged for _____!

However, the third servant made choices based in fear.

➜ Go to the Word: Read Matthew 25:24-30.

The man was only given one talent—a smaller amount than what the other servants were given, yet still a substantial sum.

How exactly does this servant describe his fears?

From how the master responded, how would you explain the reason for his disappointment with this servant?

⌁ Go to the Word: *Read James 4:17 and copy it below.*

The third servant was considered unfaithful, not only because he made no attempt to utilize what was given to him, but because he did not know his master well enough to understand his wishes. He took an opportunity his master entrusted him with, and he squandered it. Instead of taking a risk and gleaning a reward, he risked nothing. Therefore, he gained nothing. More than that, he lost his position and his standing with his master.

Just like the master, the Lord has given each of us a set of particular resources—time, material goods, skills, and abilities. We have been entrusted with these things for one reason, and that is to multiply God's investment in us for His kingdom!

What gifts or abilities has the Lord given to you?

How has fear kept you from using what God has given you for His kingdom?

Does fear have a hold on you now? How can you exchange your fear for joy today?

PRAYER FOR ABUNDANCE

Lay your fears out before God in prayer. Ask Him to help you to trust Him more.

Day Two

JOSHUA AND CALEB
Numbers 13–14

I remember the day I found out I would be writing this study—that it would be published and people would actually read it! The Lord dropped into my lap something I had been asking of Him! He was blessing our ministry in a way we had been praying for, for so long! Yet in the excitement for what was to come, I felt fear. Fear of failure—that I wasn't good enough, or smart enough, or godly enough to do what He was asking. God, in all His mega awesomeness, had given me a task that He had been preparing me for, and every instinct in me wanted to run in the other direction.

Go to the Word: *Read Numbers 13:1–25.*

In Numbers 13, Moses was instructed by the Lord to send a group of men to scout out the land promised to the descendants of Israel. One man from each tribe was selected, amounting to twelve in all. These men went to explore the land, but mostly to evaluate the people they would be displacing.

The people there were living in cities, had farmed land, and owned impressive vineyards. The scouts went into the land during the time when the grapes would be harvested. To show the abundance of the land, and their own courage, the spies returned with a cluster of grapes so huge it had to be carried on a pole between two men.

What has the Lord shown you as a promise of abundance?

What has your response been to His promises in the past?

Go to the Word: Read Numbers 13:26-14:4.

Ten of the spies were fearful of the prospect of conquering the land—they spoke about the giants there. Their descriptions filled the Israelites with fear.

Summarize in your own words what the Israelites complained about and what they wanted to do.

Go to the Word: Read the song of praise the Israelites sang to the Lord in Exodus 15:1-18.

What are some of the things the Israelites sang about the Lord that stand out to you (especially in contrast to Numbers 14:1-4)?

God had been faithful to fulfill His promises, but the power of fear had taken hold, causing the Israelites to think that it would be better to return to a life of slavery.

━━ **Go to the Word:** *Read what Joshua said to the Israelites in Numbers 14:5–10.*

Caleb and Joshua did not state that the other spies were exaggerating, though that might have been the easiest way to dispel the people's fears. Instead, they simply spoke in faith that, even with giants in the land, it was possible to defeat them with the Lord fighting for Israelites.

Look at Numbers 14:7–9. What guarantees and instructions did Joshua give to the Israelites?

Joshua and Caleb were bold because they trusted that the God of Israel was greater than the giants of Canaan. The other spies simply used their fears as a reason to not take the blessing that the Lord had given them. God had promised that the land would be theirs, if they would simply follow Him.

The majority of the spies stated that the people could not conquer the land. Only two stated that the Lord was able to do it—they were speaking an unpopular idea (the whole community wanted to stone them!), but it didn't change the truth.

Has believing in God's promises and following Jesus ever made you feel as though you were in the minority? How have you dealt with that?

The direct route into the Promised Land would have taken only eleven days for the Israelites to travel (Deuteronomy 1:2). But because of fear and doubt, an entire generation of Israelites missed out on the abundance the Lord had for them. Instead, they spent forty years wandering in the desert and died without ever experiencing the Promised Land.

Imagine the rich abundance the Lord has in store for you. How can you take the direct route into His abundance today?

PRAYER FOR ABUNDANCE

Fear caused the Israelites to forget about God's faithfulness. In your prayer time today, remember every good thing God has done for you in this past week. Ask God to protect your heart from fear and to give you courage to trust in Him.

Day Three

GIDEON LEADS AN ARMY
Judges 6–7

In his second letter to the Corinthians, Paul writes about jars that are made from common earthen clay but are used to hold something extraordinary (2 Corinthians 4:7). There is power in the glory of the Lord, and the Lord has chosen to house that amazing power inside of us. Once, He appeared to people in a temple on earth, but now His people *are* His temple. His fearful, imperfect, insecure people.

When we take the steps along the path the Lord has for us, the power of the Holy Spirit resides within us to accomplish God's tasks. The life of Jesus is made visible to the world through our actions (2 Corinthians 4:11). How sweet it is to be invited into ministry by the One who saves and restores; to be entrusted with His work!

As we often are, Gideon was filled with insecurities. His people had been beaten down, his family was considered the weakest in his tribe, and he was the youngest in the family. To any outside observer, Gideon was not leadership material. If we had met him as he was at the beginning of this story from Judges 6, we would not have believed that he would lead an army to victory.

✍ **Go to the Word:** *Read Judges 6:1–11.*

Gideon was found threshing wheat in the winepress. What was significant about that?

Threshing was tossing the grain into the air and letting the breeze carry away the chaff (think about the thin shells in popcorn that get stuck in your teeth). This was normally done on a threshing floor, which was open to the air with no walls or obstructions. However, a winepress was like a big walled-in pit.

During the time of this story, the Midianites had oppressed the Israelites, attacking them over and over again so that the Israelites were left with nothing. When the Israelites tried to raise crops, the Midianites would ride into town after the harvest and steal all the grain. By threshing grain in the winepress, Gideon was hidden and could potentially keep some grain from being stolen, instead of advertising his efforts on an open threshing floor.[1] This seems smart, but what it reveals is that Gideon had completely lost hope.

Go to the Word: *Read Judges 6:12-16.*

You can hear Gideon's despair in his reply to the angel. He did not think there would be an answer to the problems of his people—he had just learned to live with the reality that the Midianites would keep oppressing them. The Lord, however, had promised that, if His people cried out to Him, He would save them (Psalm 50:15).

What does the angel—also considered to be an appearance of the Lord Himself—challenge Gideon to do in Judges 6:14?

Gideon had to make a choice. Would he remain in despair, or would he trust that the Lord would do what He had promised to do?

Sometimes the Lord will use you in ways beyond what you think you are capable of. By doing this, He demonstrates to us that it is the Lord who accomplishes His work—we are just His vessels. As Paul described it, we are just containers for God's power.

Go to the Word: Read through the rest of Judges 6 and all of Judges 7. In each of the situations given below, note why that situation could have induced fear and how the Lord showed Himself faithful in each instance.

The angel of the Lord appears to Gideon (6:11–24).
What's scary about this?

How is God faithful?

Gideon tears down the altar to Baal and the Asherah pole (6:25–32).
What's scary about this?

How is God faithful?

God thins out Gideon's troops (7:1–8).
What's scary about this?

How is God faithful?

Gideon attacks the Midianites (7:15–23).
   What's scary about this?

How is God faithful?

Not only did the Lord give the victory to Gideon, but He did it against all odds! To defeat a large, well-supplied army with only three hundred men wielding trumpets and torches highlights the power of God. The glory of God was made visible through Gideon's actions.

Go to the Word: Read 1 Corinthians 1:26–31.

What three kinds of people did God choose?

What is the part of yourself you would consider your great weakness?

Even in our weaknesses, God chooses to use us to point to the One who created us and empowered us with the Holy Spirit in order to accomplish that which we never thought possible! The Lord used Moses, a timid man and a criminal on the run, to lead a nation (Exodus 4:10). Sarah laughed at God's promise of a child, but she bore a son in her old age (Genesis 21:6-7). Saul, a hater of Christians, became the first missionary to the Gentiles (Acts 9:15).

Insecurity can keep us from accomplishing great things by His power: *Who am I that the Lord would use me?* But the Lord has chosen us—the weak ones, the foolish ones, the ones who could not muster the power—to do His good works. Then the source of our power is unmistakable: the God of all creation is within us.

What limitations do you place on the Lord? Is there something that the Lord is calling you to accomplish that you're afraid of doing? What is it?

PRAYER FOR ABUNDANCE

God was with Gideon every step of the way, and as a result, Gideon's confidence and trust in the Lord grew. Today, ask God to bring you peace and remind you of His strength—the same strength that filled Gideon.

Day Four
PETER DENIES JESUS
Luke 22

Do you ever wish you had the kind of confidence and unabashed boldness that our children often display? Granted, it sometimes results in significant embarrassment, but the blatant honesty our children possess is really quite refreshing if you think about it.

My girls love to belt out Sunday school songs while rolling through the aisles of Target. Recently my oldest shared with the masses her rendition of "I've Got the Joy, Joy, Joy, Joy." If I'm being honest, even though there is a large part of me that is proud of them and their excitement for the gospel, a small part of me shies away from the attention they draw. In our current cultural climate, especially living where we do, I am often tempted to hush my girls for fear of condemnation.

I have fears that suppress any desire or urging I have to share the gospel. Sometimes, either directly or indirectly, I am put in the same position as Peter once was, having to respond to the challenge: "Do you know what the deal is with this Jesus guy?" What is my answer? What would your answer be? Will we live in boldness or shy away from displaying the abundance Christ offers?

I thank the Lord daily for my daughter Hannah and the example her young heart is to mine. She often asks when meeting new people, "Mommy, do they know my Jesus?" There is a reason Jesus said, "Let the little children come to me, and don't stop them, because the kingdom of God belongs to such as these" (Luke 18:16).

Peter did display boldness at the Last Supper and in the garden with Jesus, but when Jesus was later on trial, he buckled under the pressure. Let's look at what we can learn from his story.

⟿ **Go to the Word:** *Look up the verses below and note Peter's initial responses to Jesus as recorded in each of the four gospels.*

Matthew 26:33–35

Mark 14:29–31

Luke 22:33–34

John 13:36–38

In all of these passages, we see a bold and passionate statement from Peter. He stated that he would never forsake Jesus. Jesus was his friend. They traveled together for years, experiencing so many things together. Peter was part of Jesus' inner circle. He witnessed things the others did not. He acknowledged Jesus' place, enthroned in heaven. He declared that Jesus was the Son of God and the way of salvation.

In light of all this, I think we can understand Peter getting upset when Jesus states that Peter will betray Him. "Who? Me? What?! How could You say that, Jesus? That doesn't make any sense! I would die for You; I would do anything for You! I have promised to go where You go. I have promised to follow You, remember?"

And yet, the accusation of Peter's coming betrayal is one of the few incidents that is recorded in every gospel.

Go to the Word: Look up the following verses and read about Peter's denials: Matthew 26:73-75; Mark 14:69-70; Luke 22:54-57; and John 18:13-27.

In these accounts, Jesus was actively on trial, facing hostile accusers. Peter, when confronted publicly by a slave girl, could not maintain his commitment to the Lord Jesus. He folded like a cheap lawn chair. Two of the accounts even specifically note that he swore an oath that he did not know Jesus.

So what was his motivation for this denial? Obviously he was fearful of the ramifications of being counted with Jesus. But compare this to just a few hours earlier, when Peter took a sword and cut off the ear of one of the men coming for Jesus (John 18:10). In the garden, Peter had been so bold. When standing with Jesus and the others, Peter felt confident. However, when he was standing outside where Jesus' trial was taking place, Peter was in a place of fear and weakness. Why?

Recount a time when you were afraid to share the truth of Jesus. What was the cause of your fear?

As Peter stood outside, knowing the man he had been following for years was on trial for His life, it's likely Peter was not just afraid of what might happen to himself at the hands of the Romans. Peter had believed Jesus was the Son of God, the Messiah. But, what if He wasn't?

Sometimes what holds us back from proclaiming Jesus as Lord to others is not just our fear of what might happen to us as a result, but perhaps we allow doubt to creep into our hearts and minds. *Is what I believe about Jesus really true?*

Peter's faith was at stake. We have read the passages where Jesus foretold Peter's denials, but Jesus also revealed what force was at work behind the scenes.

 Go to the Word: *Read Luke 22:31–32.*

What did Jesus tell Peter (Simon) to look out for?

Jesus said that Satan had requested to sift Peter. But Jesus also had prayed for Peter to hold on to his faith. And when Peter had come back to that faith, he would be able to encourage the other disciples.

It's comforting to know that none of the details of Peter's denials surprised Jesus. He knew the intensity of the temptation that would grip Peter, and He knew that there was redemption and a plan for Peter in the future. In the same way, the Lord knows our hearts and minds. He knows our weaknesses.

*⟶ **Go to the Word:*** *Write down 1 Peter 5:8. Highlight Peter's directive to the reader.*

Peter wrote these words much later in his life, when he had learned to have a proper perspective on temptation. However, he still acknowledged the intensity of the acts of Satan.

As Paul writes, the Lord's strength is shown to be perfect through our weakness, and when we are weak, we are strong in the Lord (2 Corinthians 12:9-10). Even in weakness there is strength; there is abundance.

PRAYER FOR ABUNDANCE

Ask the Lord to reveal to you the weaknesses that keep you from being bold in your faith.

Group Discussion

STARTER

Share one story about a time when one of your children demonstrated boldness or confidence that was humbling (or embarrassing) to you.

REVIEW

1. Are you feeling defeated like Gideon was at the start of his story? How is fear causing you to miss out on the abundant life God has for you?

2. Think about a situation or an action that has been brought to your attention repeatedly in the recent past. What is the Lord calling you to do but fear is holding you back from moving forward? Why are you afraid?

3. In day four, we had you think about a time when you were afraid to share the truth of Jesus. If you feel comfortable,

share your story with the group. Discuss ways we can all become more comfortable sharing the gospel.

4. How do you think we could help each other remember the ways God has been faithful to us? How could we encourage each other?

5. How can you take the "direct route" into abundance today? What rich abundance can you imagine the Lord has in store for you?

PRAYER FOR ABUNDANCE

Let each person write down on a scrap of paper, using just a few words, a source of fear that is relevant for her. Shuffle the papers, and then pass out each one. As you pray together, ask God to root out those fears and overcome them through His faithfulness.

Room to Reflect

ABUNDANT RELATIONSHIPS

By a show of hands, how many of us feel lonely sometimes? How many feel the need for genuine community? If we were sitting together doing this study and took a quick poll, I'd venture to guess most of us feel some measure of loneliness. Motherhood can be a lonely phase of life.

I was one of the first of my friends to start having kids, and I remember feeling a sense of separation. Even as more friends began starting their families, everyone handled parenthood in her own way. Routines were different, discipline looked different, traditions were different, and so on. But the commonality of Christ can unite us in a way nothing else can.

Relationships are God's gift to us. He doesn't want us to live this life alone! He's even armed us with a handbook on relationships; you guessed it, the Bible. We are given example after example of relationships, both good and bad—examples to inspire us but also to warn us against pitfalls. I mean, we are human after all. And being human comes with many imperfections: selfishness and anger, just to name a couple. Perhaps no one is a better example of human imperfections affecting relationships than David, the king of Israel. This week, we will look at relationships through the lens of David's life.

Day One

FRIENDSHIPS AND COMMUNITY
1 Samuel 18–20; John 15:13–15

I am extremely blessed to have a fantastic community of women and moms through our church. We have fully embraced the idea of "doing life together." There have been countless meals brought, prayers said, kids babysat, outfits borrowed, Bible studies completed, along with book clubs, playdates, and supper clubs. We lift one another up when life is bringing us down. Through the good times and the hard stuff, we point one another back to Jesus. We help one another remember God's promises and Christ's sacrifice for us. When you are reminded to keep an eternal perspective, growing laundry piles and screaming kids feel less overwhelming.

This makes me think of Exodus 17:12, where we find the Israelites battling the Amalekites. Moses was instructed to hold his arms up in the air and the Israelites would win the battle. After a while, Aaron and Hur notice Moses struggling to keep his arms raised. They go to Moses and hold his arms up for him when he can no longer do it himself. I absolutely love this picture of friendship and faithfulness to uplift and encourage one another!

In this week's study, we're going to focus on another Bible hero—David. One of the most well-known examples of friendship in the Bible is the bond between David and Jonathan, who was the son of David's rival, King Saul.

Go to the Word: *Review David and Jonathan's relationship as seen in 1 Samuel 18:1–16; 19:1–7; 20:1–42.*

Jonathan was not a likely friend for David for several reasons. From the chronology, Jonathan is thought to have been at least ten years older than David and was possibly even older. David was still a "youth," not quite old enough to be in the army, and possibly in his late teens.

As we mentioned, Jonathan was also the son of the seated king of Israel, next in line for the throne. Yet David, a youngest son from the small town of Bethlehem, was the one who received the anointing from the prophet Samuel to be the next king (1 Samuel 16:10–13)! Jonathan became David's rival for the throne. Awkward! However, Jonathan respected David and seemed to respect the choice of the Lord in electing David.

Jonathan even protected David from Saul's hostility. Though David had never threatened Saul, the king sought David's life. Jonathan deceived his own father in order for David to escape, and he swore a vow to David despite his father's feelings (1 Samuel 18:1–4; 20:12–17).

*✐ **Go to the Word:** Read Proverbs 18:24, then rewrite the verse in your own words.*

Recall a person (or people) you know who could be described as the kind of friend who is closer than family. Why are you so close?

David loved Jonathan. The two friends had a closer bond than even brothers. Though Saul's dynasty would end with his death and the death of his sons, David sought to help and to protect whatever remained of his friend's family. After being established as king over a united Israel, David searched for an offspring of Jonathan to bless.

Go to the Word: *Read 2 Samuel 9.*

David found a man named Mephibosheth, Jonathan's son. He had only been five when Jonathan died, and in the haste to flee after the house of Saul had fallen, his nurse had dropped him. He was unable to walk from then on (2 Samuel 4:4).

Why do you think David sought out Mephibosheth?

Read 2 Samuel 9:9–13. How did David keep his promise to his friend Jonathan, long since dead, to care for his descendants?

Go to the Word: *Read John 15:13–15.*

How did Jesus show His disciples that He regarded them as His friends?

As you think about David and Jonathan and about how Jesus was with His disciples, what would you list as qualities of a relationship of abundance?

PRAYER FOR ABUNDANCE

If you have close friends now, thank God for those relationships. If you don't have any close friends, ask God to help you seek out healthy community.

Day Two
MARRIAGE
1 Samuel 25; 2 Samuel 11

My husband and I have had the pleasure of walking through premarital counseling with couples soon to head down the aisle. One thing we talk about is the idea that there is no perfect person. There is no such thing as "the one," as much as "the one *for you*." If you keep looking for a perfect person, you'll never stop looking.

Marriage is a choice, a commitment, made by two sinful people. We can guarantee they will hurt each other at some point, probably far deeper than anyone else in their lives could. There is a vulnerability in marriage that requires a complete revealing of oneself, which in turn requires trust. I have experienced a marriage that ended in betrayal and a loving marriage marked by grace and abundance. Though my first marriage is a story I often wish was never told, I can see purpose in it. That experience is part of what led me to my husband and children. I have a first-hand perspective on divorce that has served me well in ministry.

God can take our mess and redeem it for His glory! And whether you are married or single now, if you put God first and keep trusting in His faithfulness, He will take the experiences of your life and use them to help you grow into a person who loves and serves others in healthy, abundant relationships.

David's life, again, provides an example for us of God's redemptive power in our relationships. David may have been a wonderful friend, but he was not an exemplary husband. He had a number of wives and concubines, something that would have been expected at the time. As the king, he was to produce heirs and show his power through his large family.

Of course, we now know, and Scripture supports the fact, that God's ideal is one man and one woman for marriage. However, we can use these examples from David's marriages to learn more about the heart of God, and to recognize the pitfalls of relationships that do not honor God.

David's first wife was one who had been promised to him because of his courage in facing a certain giant (1 Samuel 17:25).

Go to the Word: *Read about how David's first marriage came about in 1 Samuel 18:20-30.*

What were the reasons Saul had for giving his daughter to David?

Go to the Word: *Read 1 Chronicles 3:1–9.*

List the other wives David had, as seen in this genealogical record. What are their names and how are they described?

 1.

 2.

 3.

 4.

 5.

 6.

 7.

We don't know much about all of David's wives, but given the culture of the time and David's role, it would be fair to say that many of these relationships were born out of a particular purpose other than romantic love—whether for creating unions between powerful households and regions, or for simply producing many offspring to support and carry on David's legacy.

What do you think the purpose of marriage is today?

Two of David's wives are recorded as having pivotal roles in shaping the character or life of David. One of those wives is Abigail. Let's walk through the scriptures and learn a little about her.

Go to the Word: Read about Abigail from 1 Samuel 25.

What does 1 Samuel 25:2-3 tell us about Abigail?

From the same verses, who is her husband and how is he described?

David and his servants were in the wilderness when David sent his men to the wealthy Nabal to ask for help. Nabal was incredibly disrespectful to them; accused them of being runaway, unfaithful servants; and sent them away with nothing (verses 4–11).

When David heard of Nabal's response, what was his reaction (verses 13, 21–22)?

One of Nabal's servants was wise enough to tell Abigail about Nabal's foolish response to David's men. Make a list of all the things Abigail gathered secretly to offer David and his men (verses 14–19).

In addition to all these things, we see in verses 23–31 that Abigail offered David one more thing: respect. List some of the actions and words of Abigail that reflected her respect for David and for God.

Abigail not only gives David respect, but she also takes Nabal's shame upon herself. David is so impressed, he spares Nabal and praises the Lord because of Abigail. A skirmish was avoided, but Nabal didn't even know what was going on because he was back at home in a drunken stupor. When he awoke from his stupor and was told about the danger he had avoided, Nabal suffered from something like a heart attack or a stroke, and died ten days later.

How did David respond to this news according to verses 39–42?

David saw virtue in Abigail and saw her wisdom and perseverance, even in a terrible relationship. The Lord was the One who judged her husband, and Abigail was free from Nabal through his death. The Lord made her available, and David married her.

The marriage of David and Bathsheba, however, came about under much different circumstances. The events of this story prove to be one of the low points of David's life. His actions and decisions at this time resulted in terrible consequences. But let's see what the Lord does, in spite of David's behavior.

Go to the Word: Read 2 Samuel 11.

According to the first verse of this chapter, what time of year was It?

As king, where should David have been at that time?

David looked out from the roof of his palace and saw a woman bathing in the evening. Rather than stop looking, what did he do (verses 3-4)?

David committed adultery. As the Scriptures say, "your sin will catch up with you" (Numbers 32:23). Bathsheba was soon found to be carrying David's child, while her husband, Uriah, was off to war.

In your own words, summarize what David did to Uriah (verses 6–17)?

After Bathsheba had finished mourning for her husband, David made her his wife. What did the Lord think of this (verse 27)?

In the next chapter, the prophet Nathan confronted David. Nathan told him a story to illustrate the nature of his sin.

Go to the Word: Read 2 Samuel 12:1–14.

What did Nathan say the Lord would do to David to punish him for his sin?

Take a moment to compare this story with that of David and Abigail. David went from being part of the answer to a woman's prayer to being the source of a woman's pain. Bathsheba suffered great loss because of the sinful relationship with David—first her husband, then her child (verses 15–18). But hope would be found in another child—Solomon.

David, Bathsheba, and Solomon ended up becoming part of the family line of Jesus Christ (Matthew 1).

What does that say about how the Lord can redeem people and relationships?

Go to the Word: Read Genesis 2:24 and 1 Corinthians 6:15–16.

Based on these verses, what is God's intention for marriage?

God designed marriage to create a union with two lives— a man and a woman. True abundance in that relationship is made possible in being satisfied in what the Lord has given as a pattern.

If the two are made one through marriage, then what do you think are some good results of that kind of relationship?

PRAYER FOR ABUNDANCE

Think about the relationships you have had and the ways you have been blessed through them. If you are in a marriage now, ask God to help you to continue to focus on His purpose for your relationship with your husband. If you are not married, consider how God might use you to help support and encourage healthy, abundant relationships in your life.

Day Three

CHILDREN

2 Samuel 13–15; 1 Kings 1–2

Our children have the ability to be both our greatest joy and our greatest sorrow, often at the same time. If you are a mom, you know what I mean. This is true during just about any stage of your child's life. Whether your young child lied to you for the first time or your teenager sneaked out for the hundredth time, you have to fight to find abundance in parenthood. There is, indeed, a bond between mother and child that can become a difficult roadblock between us and God at times.

The idea of God giving His Son to die resonates in such a different way when you are a parent. When you turn it around and think of yourself giving up your child for the lives of many—it feels unthinkable. God made this huge sacrifice for us so that we might have eternal life and experience the glorious abundance only He can give! We will never experience full abundance in our relationships with our children without understanding the example of our heavenly Father.

King David, son of Jesse, was father to nineteen children, according to the Scriptures. Two additional sons died in infancy, and one daughter, Tamar, is named in the Bible. David's first-born son, Amnon, would have been next in line for the throne.

Go to the Word: *Read 2 Samuel 13:1–15 to see how Amnon's love for his sister turned into sin.*

This is a horrible and inexcusable action. How could this happen? The heart of man is desperately wicked and has a persistent potential for sin and rebellion.

How did David respond to this horrendous behavior by his son? All we are told is that he was furious (verse 21). Tamar went to live with her brother Absalom in his house. But Amnon apparently stayed in the king's household. And Absalom hated Amnon for what he did to his sister.

David seemed to fail to act appropriately as a father and a leader here. Perhaps he looked the other way because Amnon was his firstborn. Whatever the reason, this passivity allowed sin to go unchecked.

Go to the Word: *Read Proverbs 13:24.*

How does this verse describe the one who disciplines his child?

Many people have misinterpreted this verse to mean that we should punish our children by beating them with rods. However, "the rod" in biblical times would have been understood as a reference to the rod that shepherds would use to guide and redirect straying sheep. The proverb writer is using the rod as a symbol of loving discipline administered by parents—a symbol that would have been familiar to his readers—not as an instruction for physical punishment.

David did not guide his children in this terrible situation. He did not help to bring about repentance or forgiveness or discipline.

Go to the Word: *Read about the results of Amnon's acts that came about two years afterward: 2 Samuel 13:23–33.*

What did Absalom do to Amnon?

Absalom was the third born, but he was David's initial choice to succeed him. He wanted Absalom to take the throne and live uprightly. He wanted a peaceful succession with his son. However, this was not to be. Remember, the Lord had promised that "the sword" would never leave David's house because of David's deeds with Bathsheba and Uriah (2 Samuel 12:10).

Beginning in 2 Samuel 15, we see that Absalom was plotting what would become a violent uprising to forcibly take the throne from his aging father. His plan included not only seeking to kill his father but also humiliating him and accomplishing unspeakable acts against his father's household out in the open for all Israel to see (2 Samuel 16:20–22). Absalom was showing that he was now not only king but the sole head of the household as well.

Go to the Word: *Read Proverbs 22:6, then rephrase it in your own words.*

While David's errant training of his sons was not the only factor in their sinful behavior, it is clear that David's zeal for the Lord and His justice, as seen in the slaying of Goliath (1 Samuel 17), did not translate well to his own family.

David had seen what his son was capable of and what unchecked sin accomplishes in the heart. The time came when the two would have to confront each other. When David's troops went out to fight Absalom's, David ordered his men not to hurt Absalom.

*➤ **Go to the Word:** Read about Absalom's end in 2 Samuel 18:9–17 and David's response in verse 33.*

Does David's response surprise you? Why, or why not?

After Absalom's death, David eventually regained control of the throne. First Kings 1 records events toward the end of David's life. At this point, the king was quite old and frail. The people were anxious to see who would be king after David. Absalom's younger brother Adonijah began to assert himself as being the heir to David, and he tried to push his way onto the throne while David was weak and lying in his bed.

*➤ **Go to the Word:** First Kings 1:15–35 records a conversation between Bathsheba and David concerning these events.*

According to this passage, what had David already promised to Bathsheba concerning David's heir?

Go to the Word: Read 1 Kings 1:38–40.

What event sealed Solomon as being the next king of Israel?

We don't know what kind of father that David was to his children. He wrote about the fear and worship of God in many of the psalms, but he seems to have missed opportunities to instill that reverence for the Lord in his children. But, in spite of the sins of His servants, the Lord was faithful to keep His promises to David in maintaining a son on the throne.

Go to the Word: Read 1 Kings 2:1–4. Restate David's last words to Solomon in your own words.

PRAYER FOR ABUNDANCE

Consider what your goals are for your relationships with your
children. Ask God to help you to see what you need to do to
guide them into abundant life with Him.

Day Four

FAITHFULNESS AND LEGACY
2 Samuel 7

For this study, let's go back in time in David's life to just after David had brought the ark of the covenant to Jerusalem. He desired that the capital of Israel be made God's holy city, a place designed for worship.

Go to the Word: Read 2 Samuel 7:1-17.

What was David thinking about in this passage?

As David was contemplating these things, what promises from the Lord were spoken to Nathan the prophet?

How did God describe David's dynasty in verse 16?

These words of permanence were unheard of in David's day. Royal houses were places of intrigue and drama, with different factions vying for the throne. Even in David's own court there had been at least two attempts to overthrow him, coming from his own sons. Just imagine the plans of other monarchies in other lands where even more immorality was being practiced!

But to David, God made an enduring promise: a permanent dynasty, established forever. How could this ever be accomplished, though?

David had desired to build a physical house for God to be worshipped in. The Lord stated that David would not be the man to do this because his reign had been marked with the spilling of blood and warfare. His successor, a man of peace, would then be permitted to build the temple. This was Solomon. But because of David's heart to serve the Lord, God instead promised David an eternal household.

Who in David's line to come would embody this eternal dynasty?

*✍ **Go to the Word:** Read Jeremiah 23:5–6.*

According to the prophet Jeremiah, who would the Lord raise up?

During the time of Jeremiah, the people of Israel were oppressed and under threat of invasion and destruction. To hear about a king who would bring justice and righteousness back to the land must have brought wonderful hope during the nation's most difficult time!

How do you communicate the hope of Jesus in your relationships?

2— Go to the Word: Read Matthew 21:8-11.

What is Jesus called in this passage?

Who was declaring this?

2— Go to the Word: Read John 19:1-22.

What was the charge brought against Jesus—the official reason for His execution?

~~ ***Go to the Word:*** *Read Revelation 5:1–5, describing some of John's vision of heaven.*

Who is being named in verse 5, and what is He said to have done?

~~ ***Go to the Word:*** *Read Revelation 22:16.*

How does Jesus describe Himself?

David was promised that a descendant would sit on the throne forever. The only person who could ever fulfill this promise was Jesus Himself. This promised eternity brought hope to Israel in dark times, and it still brings hope to us today.

The Lord wants to have an abundant relationship with you. No matter what you have done or have had done to you, the Lord knows. He wants you to rest and trust in Him that He will work all things together for your good. If you are trusting in the eternal Lord to save you from your sins based on His merit and not your own, then Jesus is your King.

This relationship may have come through David, but it now extends far beyond David's family. All people are invited to taste and see that the Lord is good, to fall before His throne, to worship Him, and to follow Him as servants of King Jesus. And all people can have the hope of an eternal legacy.

PRAYER FOR ABUNDANCE

Praise Jesus as your King!

Group Discussion

STARTER

Talk about a relationship you had with a mother (either your own mother or another person) that meant a lot to you. What did you learn from that relationship?

REVIEW

1. Are you currently in a place of loneliness and craving community? Describe the relationships and community you desire. Discuss Proverbs 18:24.

2. How have you experienced or extended grace in your marriage? What are some unselfish ways you can show grace to your spouse? And, if you are not married, talk about what you have learned from examples of good marriages in your life.

3. Talk about David's passivity toward his children's behavior. What can we learn from his relationship with his children?

4. How should we think about discipline as part of an abundant relationship with our children?

5. David was promised an eternal legacy. What kind of legacy do you hope to create in your family?

PRAYER FOR ABUNDANCE

Let everyone share needs related to their relationships with the people in their lives. Pray over these needs for one another. Ask God to show you clearly how to pursue abundance in relationships.

Room to Reflect

A NEW PERSPECTIVE

Often, we hear references to God doing "exceedingly abundantly above all that we ask or think" (Ephesians 3:20 NKJV). Throughout Scripture, we see God blessing people and promising blessings to people. Even some of Proverbs talks about ways to be prosperous. It can get a little tricky when we talk about abundant life and blessings, and then we wonder: Is prosperity a sign of abundant life?

Abundance is not always what we think.

Let's take Hebrews 11, for example. Here we get a highlight reel of the great people of faith—but many of these people were tortured, imprisoned, stoned, mistreated, homeless, and they faced many other trials. While they experienced great blessings from God, they also endured many hardships.

Even Paul, the author of the phrase "exceedingly abundantly," did most of his writing about joy and peace right in the middle of some incredibly difficult circumstances. But still, he would say that Christ was enough for him.

Abundant life is not about what we have or what we get. It's not about what we do or what our current circumstances look like. Abundant life is about the free gift we receive from the Lord and what happens when we live as good stewards of that blessing. As we wrap up our final week of study, let's focus on this mind-set. Abundance should give us a new perspective on our lives and the way we do everything, because we have been transformed by Jesus Christ!

Day One

IT'S NOT ABOUT WHAT YOU HAVE

Psalm 37:4; James 1:17

When I was a little girl, I wanted a Barbie Dreamhouse more than anything. On the morning of my seventh birthday, I woke up to find all my little girl dreams had come true. There sat a gorgeous three-story mansion complete with an elevator, beautifully detailed furniture, and even a bright pink convertible parked out front.

My life was complete. At least for my seven-year-old self.

However, as life has it, the hot pink faded on the convertible and the elevator stopped working, and soon the dream world wasn't what it used to be. But I had new dreams as I grew. I wanted to fill my life with more and more things to make me happy.

I then became an adult, and the dreams of my three-story Barbie Dreamhouse morphed into a life-size dream house, with just as many amenities as that plastic world had had. Not much had really changed from my seven-year-old perspective after all.

Go to the Word: Read Psalm 37:4: "Take delight in the LORD, and he will give you your heart's desires."

I first heard Psalm 37:4 when I was a teenager. I clung to that verse and made it my anthem. *Lord, I will follow You and You'll give me everything I want! The real-life Barbie Dreamhouse! The perfect husband! My dream job! My life will be great!*

But I was hearing that verse all wrong. As I began to read and study my Bible more and more through college, I learned that the verse I had claimed as my "life verse" did not mean exactly what I thought it did.

What does Psalm 37:4 mean to you?

God may give you all the desires of your heart—but He might not. If you are delighting yourself in Him, He will shape your heart's desires to be like His desires. You will delight in the things that also delight God.

So, when you don't wake up in your Barbie Dreamhouse, you'll realize it doesn't matter, because there's still abundant life in Him, no matter what material things you have.

Because I want you to understand Scripture correctly and not claim a life verse just because it sounds appealing (like I did), let's take a deeper look at this specific verse. In this psalm, David is calling us to delight in the Lord and commit everything we do to Him. This psalm is a Hebrew poem, and the word translated "delight" (עָנַג, pronounced aw-nag)[1] literally means "to be delicate or feminine." It is the idea of being pliable or sensitive. In this context, the word means "to be dependent on God and to derive your pleasure from Him."

Does this describe you? Do you derive your greatest pleasure from God alone? Where do you go first when you want to find happiness—to God or somewhere else?

The psalmist called us to delight ourselves in the Lord—this wasn't a suggestion. The way this verb is translated in Hebrew makes it a command! But how can you delight in God? A couple of ways in our busy culture are to make Him our primary pleasure (easier said than done anymore, right?) and to find contentment with the things we already have.

Go to the Word: *The following scriptures help us delight in the Lord; write them out below.*

Matthew 22:37

John 15:7

Are you content with your home? Your car? Your clothes? Your children? Rate (from 0 to 100) what percentage of time you spend thinking about how you'd like to change the "things" in your life and feeling frustrated with what you have.

0%   50%   100%

How much time do you spend living in abundance and being grateful for what you have?

0%   50%   100%

Pause for a moment, then write out a prayer of thankfulness to God for all of the blessings you do have:

Okay, so what about financial blessings? If prosperity isn't a sign of abundance, is it wrong to have a lot? I think it's more about how we use what we have.

I saw a framed picture once that read "When you have more than you need, build a longer table, not a higher fence." That has always stuck with me. When God blesses you with much, give much away. Be willing to open your doors and let others in.

We can't always get hung up on money when we hear "prosperous," though.

Go to the Word: Read James 1:17: *"Every good and perfect gift is from above, coming down from the Father of lights, who does not change like shifting shadows."*

Abundance isn't about what we have; it's about what we do with what we are given. We want to be thankful for what God has given us and recognize how God blesses others. This will shift our hearts toward contentment and away from coveting.

How is God blessing those around you?

PRAYER FOR ABUNDANCE

Thank God for how He has blessed people you know. Ask God to guard your heart against jealousy and to help you take delight where He delights.

Day Two

IT'S NOT ABOUT WHAT YOU DO

Matthew 23:11–12; 1 Corinthians 13:11–12

I'm a doer. A busy bee. I work all day until I'm bone tired, and then I usually plop on the couch with my computer to pound out a couple more hours of work; it's a race to see what will close first—my eyes or my laptop!

I struggle to rest, and I struggle with taking my hands off things to allow others (even God) to do some of the work. Sometimes I try to convince myself that because the work I'm doing is "good work," then it's okay. Because it's ministry, it's all right to let my priorities fall out of whack.

But then I get that nudging in my heart, that gentle reminder that I'm so zoned in on what I think is making a difference for God that I've forgotten about my own life. My own relationships. The people God has placed right there in my own house.

I think we all can relate, especially as moms. Sometimes we are doing so much for our kids, we forget to take care of ourselves (remember that airplane oxygen mask rule?). Or, if you're like me, you get more focused on *doing for* God instead of *growing in* God.

Check out this list of things that can rob you of abundant life. Circle any that are a problem for you:

Worry
Stress
Too much
Pride
Sin

Now look at the things you can do to find abundant life. Draw an arrow pointing to the ones you want to include in your life this week:

Go to God's Word first

Pray more

Have accountability with others

Rest

I can be a pastor's wife, run a ministry for women, write books, and speak to and encourage women. But none of those things will bring me abundant life. We can go on mission trips, adopt children, go to church, and post pretty Scripture images on Instagram. None of these things is bad—but none brings us closer to God by itself.

We can't allow ourselves to become too focused on the things we do for God. Abundant life is not about the things that you do—it's about growing "in the grace and knowledge of our Lord and Savior Jesus Christ" (2 Peter 3:18). Abundant life is a continuous practice of learning and maturing—as well as failing and recovering!

When I think about overdoing for God, I can't help but consider the Pharisees, the Jewish religious leaders of Jesus' day. The actual root meaning of the word *Pharisee* is "to separate or detach," and that's exactly what the Pharisees were about. They spent their lives detached from community, comparing and measuring themselves against others, always trying hard to be the best. In fact, they were Jesus' biggest persecutors.

When describing the Pharisees, Jesus said, "They do not practice what they preach. They tie up heavy, cumbersome loads and put them on other people's shoulders, but they themselves are not willing to lift a finger to move them.

Everything they do is done for people to see" (Matthew 23:3–5 NIV). The Pharisees believed they had to do certain things to measure up, and they prided themselves on being better than others because they worked so hard to follow the rules.

Go to the Word: *Read Matthew 23:11–12 to understand what Jesus said about these actions.*

Who will be the greatest among you?

What will happen to those who exalt themselves?

What will happen to those who humble themselves?

Go to the Word: *Write out 1 Corinthians 13:11–12.*

The more we grow in the grace and knowledge of Christ, the more we grow up and become more like Him and live abundantly in Him. The more we know Him, the more we set aside childish ways, such as the need to be right, or the struggle to measure up. We can begin to step out of the things that rob us of abundance and can start living in abundance. For now, we see a blurry reflection of who He truly is and who we are to be in Him. Someday we will come face to face with God and all will be made clear—our abundance will be complete!

PRAYER FOR ABUNDANCE

Ask God to help you let go of those things robbing you of your abundant life in Him this week. Pick one activity to focus on that will help you grow in the grace and knowledge of Jesus Christ. Make a promise to God that you will invest in that activity this week.

Day Three

IT'S NOT ABOUT YOUR CIRCUMSTANCES

Philippians 1

As a brand-new mom with a challenging, colicky baby at home, I decided to make some major sacrifices. Notably, I quit my busy job and became a stay-at-home mom. Somehow, once pregnancy is behind you, you forget about all the difficult parts. We wanted more kids, and we figured we might as well get it over with, so ... my husband and I had three babies in less than three years. Those early years were a whirlwind and just about broke me. I told this story in my book *Mom Up*:

> Then came the day I hurled a sippy cup of apple juice against the wall because my two-year-old couldn't clean up a mess correctly. What was happening to me? Who was this angry, self-absorbed person who couldn't even allow a child to be a child?
>
> All I could feel was shame. God had blessed me with three beautiful, healthy children— why couldn't I enjoy them? What was wrong with me? Many women would give anything to have kids, but I couldn't shake the feeling that God had somehow messed up by giving mine to me.
>
> I told myself things like:
> *Surely someone else could do a better job.*
> *I am not cut out for this.*
> *Why does joy feel a lot more like torture? ...*

People had told me, "If anyone can handle this, it's you!"—a compliment meant for encouragement that only served to make me feel guilty and "less than." I had been comparing myself with an image of a better version of me, and I let it defeat me.

When I was diagnosed with postpartum anxiety and depression, all my fears about myself came to the surface. I wasn't the ideal mom I had tried to convince myself I was. I had worked hard at holding things together, always keeping my cool....

For months and months, I went to sleep with fear and woke up exhausted, with no desire to get out of bed. My mind raced with the *what ifs* and a constant reminder of my failures. *What if I can't do this mom thing? What if I can't control myself and I hurt someone I love? What if I mess up my kids too bad? What if I'm not cut out for this to begin with?*

My dreams of motherhood were shattered, and I was falling to pieces with them.[2]

The good news is, that's just a snippet of my story, but if you keep reading, you will discover that God met me in one of the darkest seasons of my life and brought me more joy and abundance than I had ever experienced before. Abundance has nothing to do with our circumstances!

You can be sitting at the bedside of your terminally sick child—there is abundance there.

You can be watching your marriage fall apart—there is abundance there.

You can be having another fight with a stubborn teenager—there is abundance there.

You can be wondering how you will put food on the table—there is abundance there.

What circumstances in your life have left you feeling like you couldn't obtain abundant life?

The apostle Paul knew a thing or two about circumstances and what it looks like to live out the abundant life in Christ no matter what is going on. He wrote the letter to the Philippians during his first Roman imprisonment; he had planted this church about ten years prior. While Paul could have been devastated by his imprisonment, he instead wrote this letter that was full of hope. His desire was solely for Christ to be glorified through everything.

I'm not sure I could say I would be able to do the same—could you?

Go to the Word: Read Philippians 1.

Where does Paul's joy come from?

First Peter 5:5 says that "God resists the proud but gives grace to the humble." Maybe your positive circumstances are keeping you from abundant life. Maybe, unlike Paul, your life is comfortable and easy, and you are taking pride in how far you've come. Often, it's easier for us to forget our need for God when we don't *feel* like we need Him.

Paul knew that Christ was all he had and all he needed. This is why he was able to say, "For me, to live is Christ and to die is gain" (Philippians 1:21).

Take a moment to consider your circumstances: your home, your family, your schedule. Do you have the same attitude as Paul—to live is Christ and to die is gain? What would that attitude look like for you?

PRAYER FOR ABUNDANCE

As you consider your home, your family, and your schedule, give each of these things up to God. Humble yourself before Him. Ask Him to take the lead in your life.

Day Four

IT'S ABOUT WHAT WE LEAVE BEHIND
1 Corinthians 2:9

The summer before my freshman year of college, I went through "rush week," where we would interview at the different sorority houses, get to know them, and see which place would be the best fit for us during our time at college. I kept hearing this buzz about girls who had the title of "legacy." They seemed so special and unique; they always got a little extra-special treatment. But I didn't really know what that meant at the time.

Later, I asked one of the girls staying on my dorm floor what a "legacy" was, and she explained that they were the daughters or granddaughters of the sororities' alumni. On "bid day" we received a welcome to our new sisterhood, and I loved seeing these "legacies" with their moms, aunts, or grandmothers—all lined up, wearing matching colors and letters, proudly representing the house they had all been a part of through their college days. What a fun experience!

This image stuck in my head as I had my own girls and thought of the legacy I want to pass on to them—not just a love for a specific university (although I married a man from the rival university, so that will be interesting when the time comes!), but something so much more. A legacy of abundant life. We want to be women who grow in abundance so that we can pass on a legacy of abundance to our children.

➤ **Go to the Word:** *Read 1 Corinthians 2:9. Take a moment to write out this scripture and let it really sink in.*

Have you ever caught a glimpse of the love, joy, and hope God has for us? What was that like?

Our eyes, ears, and hearts can't conceive how incredible the things are that God is preparing for those of us who love Him! The word *abundant* in the Greek is *perissos*,[3] meaning "exceeding abundantly, beyond measure, very highly." Jesus promises us a life far better than we could ever imagine. It is so considerably more than what we could ever expect or anticipate. Beyond measure!

What are some material legacies you want to leave for your children?

What are the spiritual legacies you want to leave for your children?

We have big dreams and goals for our kids, but our minds are very limited in the scope of what God can and is doing for us. Imagine how much greater the plans are that God is preparing for each of us! It's mind-blowing, isn't it?

I don't know about you, but I so easily get caught up in the here-and-now and forget about the legacy that I'm leaving behind. I want well-behaved children and a clean house, when that's not the end goal at all. The end goal is to leave a legacy of abundant life to our children, and it starts with us living in it right now.

What needs to change in your life in order to walk in abundance in Christ more freely?

Imagine you are fully living the abundant life Christ promised. What does that look like? What might it look like through the eyes of your children?

Okay, friend, now it's time. You've done the work, but now you need to go and live it. Walk in abundance the way that Jesus modeled for us. Love abundantly. Live abundantly. Give abundantly. Pass on a legacy of abundance to your children!

Jesus loves you beyond measure. We have this privilege of running together in the abundant life He offers!

PRAYER FOR ABUNDANCE

Spend some time reviewing some of the verses we've read in this week's study, or go back and look at other weeks. Pick a verse that is meaningful to you and use it as your prayer for abundance today.

WEEK SIX

Group Discussion

STARTER

Think of something a parent or grandparent or other elder in your life has passed on to you. It could be a material item or a personality trait, a physical feature, or a tradition. Talk about the legacy that you have received.

REVIEW

1. Way back in the beginning of this study, we talked about what our definition of *abundance* was. Give your definition as you understand it now. Has your idea of abundance changed since the beginning of the study?

** *Abundance* is**

2. Delighting in the Lord means to be dependent on God and to derive your pleasure from Him. Does this describe you? Discuss with your group what this might look like for you, and challenge one another to find ways to delight in the Lord more.

3. If abundant life is not about doing good works, what is it about? What can you do to find abundant life? (Hint: look back at 2 Peter 3:18 and read this scripture together.)

4. What circumstances have left you feeling like you can't have abundant life? What does God's Word say about this?

5. Jesus promises us a life better than we could ever imagine, and we get to pass that on to our children! What a gift! Discuss some ways that you can create a legacy of abundance in your home.

PRAYER FOR ABUNDANCE

As you close your last group time for this study, spend extra time in prayer. Find out what struggles or burdens are weighing on the hearts of those in your group, and pray for God to lift those hardships, freeing the women in this group so they can go and live the abundant life in Christ!

Room to Reflect

LEADER GUIDE

Hello, Leaders!

Thank you for investing in the lives of the women around you! Whether this is your first time leading a Bible study or you've led many groups before, we appreciate the time and sacrifice you make for your group. We want to come alongside you and help you feel prepared to lead. Here you will find a starting-off point to help you prepare for your meeting times.

The group discussions can range from about 30–45 minutes if you are meeting in person. Below you will find a suggested outline for your group time, but feel free to tailor your time together to fit your needs.

GETTING STARTED TIPS
PRAY!!
As you are preparing to lead your group, prayer is key!! Spend time each week praying for the ladies in your group and praying that God will lead and direct your time.

FIND A LOCATION
Decide what works best for your group. Meeting at someone's house? At a coffee shop? In a local park? At a church? Online? Get some feedback. If the women in your group don't have the transportation, means, or the time to meet up somewhere—consider hosting an online Facebook group. We provide tips for how to do this at thrivemoms.com/community. If you have a really large group and can meet at your church, consider providing childcare.

PLAN AND PREPARE

Be very familiar with your material! Read through the material and make notes before your discussion time so you can make sure your time together flows smoothly.

FOLLOW UP

Take time during the week to follow up with the women in your group and check in on how they are doing. Remind them about meeting times, and encourage engagement within your group.

GROUP LEADING TIPS

BEFORE YOU MEET

Take some time to go through the week of material, and make notes on anything that you may need to clarify deeper with your group. As a leader, you need to be prepared, so make sure you have answered every question, filled in every blank, and read all of the content. Go through all of the group discussion questions, answering each one and having questions picked out that you think will be good for your group. You can also use space on the discussion pages or the Room to Reflect pages to add questions or thoughts of your own.

Keep your mind and heart open to how the Lord leads your group. You may have someone come with a question, concern, or need that may take more time than you are prepared for. Your group time may not always look the way you think, so leave room for growth. Remember that your group members are getting into the material on their own too.

PREPARE

Helping to set a comfortable and inviting atmosphere for your group is a great way to start your meeting time each week. This may be the only time during the week your women have away from their kids or (if kids are at the location) one of the few chances they have to partake in focused adult conversations that aren't all about their children or their work stress. You want them to walk in and feel a sense of peace and rest. Being a thoughtful host makes a huge difference in the atmosphere of your group and in your ability to connect with one another and the content.

Here are a few ways you can prepare for your group time:

- Pray over the room and each person attending.
- Minimize any distractions (remove sight and sound clutter as much as possible) and create a comfortable environment, with seating available for everyone. Your group will struggle to engage if they are uncomfortable and distracted.
- If you are hosting online—post ahead of time, welcoming them. Make sure your live video setup is comfortable and inviting, with clear sound and enough light.

WELCOME (10 Minutes)

As your group arrives, take some time to welcome each person and catch up briefly on what's happening in people's lives. Make any introductions or announcements you need to here. If drinks or snacks are available, invite everyone to get those before they find their seats.

DISCUSSION (20-30 Minutes)

Use the Starter question, if you wish, to begin the conversation. Sometimes, especially in groups where the members don't know one another well, it can be helpful to have a chance to talk about more everyday issues before diving into the spiritual discussion.

After a few people have responded to the Starter, move into the Review of the week's study by discussing the provided questions. If you are in the second week of the study or any week past that, it might also be helpful for you to briefly summarize the main points of the previous session (especially if some members haven't been able to make it to every meeting).

Allow people to share anything that stood out to them and to ask questions about any parts of the session they didn't understand. If you can, take notes about any specific needs or issues your group members mention so you can pray for those later.

PRAYER (5–10 Minutes)

After you complete your discussion time, build prayer into each group session. Prayer prompts are provided, or you may wish to spend some time going around and praying for the specific needs of your group members. Note pages are provided at the end of each session so people can jot down reminders of any needs they may want to continue praying over during the week. Check in with your women throughout the week and pray for them daily!

NOTES

WEEK ONE: THE WAY IT WAS MEANT TO BE

1. Kara-Kae James, *Mom Up: Thriving with Grace in the Chaos of Motherhood* (Colorado Springs: David C Cook, 2019), 42.

2. James, *Mom Up*, 43.

WEEK THREE: TIME ISN'T ALWAYS ON OUR SIDE

1. E. Randolph Richards and Brandon J. O'Brien, *Misreading Scripture with Western Eyes: Removing Cultural Blinders to Better Understand the Bible* (Downers Grove, IL: InterVarsity, 2012), 145.

2. Louis Berkhof, *Systematic Theology* (Grand Rapids, MI: Eerdmans, 1949), 262.

3. Kara-Kae James, *Mom Up: Thriving with Grace in the Chaos of Motherhood* (Colorado Springs: David C Cook, 2019), 37–38.

WEEK FOUR: DON'T LET FEAR STEAL YOUR ABUNDANCE

1. James M. Freeman and Harold J. Chadwick, *Manners and Customs of the Bible* (North Brunswick, NJ: Bridge-Logos, 1998), 96, accessed at https://ref.ly/logosres/nmncstbib?ref=Bible.Ge50.11-12&off=416&ctx=alled+Abel+Mizraim.%0a-The+threshing+floor+.

WEEK SIX: A NEW PERSPECTIVE

1. *The New Strong's Exhaustive Concordance of the Bible, Hebrew and Aramaic Dictionary of the Old Testament*, ed. James Strong (Nashville, TN: Thomas Nelson, 1995), 108.

2. Kara-Kae James, *Mom Up: Thriving with Grace in the Chaos of Motherhood* (Colorado Springs: David C Cook, 2019), 30–32.

3. *Strong's*, Greek, 70, #4053.

ABOUT THE AUTHORS

Kara-Kae James is a writer and encourager, passionate about seeing women's lives changed and impacted through the gospel. She is the founder and executive director of Thrive Moms, a ministry dedicated to seeing moms step out of survival mode and into the thriving, abundant life that God calls them to. She is also the author of the book *Mom Up: Thriving with Grace in the Chaos of Motherhood*.

Kara-Kae is married to her husband, Brook, and is a mom to four. She works daily to encourage women to reach their potential as moms and as daughters of Christ. She loves pouring into moms because she knows firsthand that many are struggling and in desperate need of a reminder that God loves us, and we are doing His holy work.

Ali Pedersen is a writer and pastor's wife who has a heart for bringing people together. She is the community director of Thrive Moms and works with women to find fellowship right where they are.

Ali is married to her husband, Nicolai, and is a mom to four girls. She spends her days creating resources for women, homeschooling her kiddos, and baking lots of cookies. She enjoys fostering community among women and creating deep relationships for the sake of the kingdom.